1979   1980   1981   1982

1983   1984   1985   1986

1987   1988   1989   1990

1991   1992   1993   1994

The Pritzker Architecture Prize: *The First Twenty Years*

1995   1996   1997   1998

JOHNSON   BARRAGÁN   STIRLING   ROCHE

PEI   MEIER   HOLLEIN   BÖHM

TANGE   BUNSHAFT   GEHRY   ROSSI
                      NIEMEYER

VENTURI   SIZA   MAKI   PORTZAMPARC

ANDO   MONEO   FEHN   PIANO

Martha Thorne, *editor*

Colin Amery

J. Carter Brown

William J. R. Curtis

Bill N. Lacy

The Pritzker Architecture Prize:

The First Twenty Years

Harry N. Abrams, Inc., Publishers,
in association with
The Art Institute of Chicago

Dedicated to the memory of Jay Pritzker, 1922–1999

Editor: Diana Murphy
Designer: Judith Hudson

Jacket front: see pages 53, 59, © Timothy
Hursley, 71, 146, 155, 161, © Terje Solvang,
courtesy Renzo Piano Building Workshop
Jacket back: see pages 79, 83, courtesy Studio
Hollein / © Sina Baniahmad, 96, 101, 107,
113, 119, 128, 133, courtesy the office of Alvaro
Siza, 143, 149

*Library of Congress Cataloging-in-
Publication Data*
The Pritzker Architecture Prize : the first
twenty years.
p.   cm.
Includes bibliographical references and index.
ISBN 0–8109–4371–9 (hardcover). —
ISBN 0–8109–2910–4 (AIC pbk.)
1. Pritzker Architecture Prize.
2. Architecture, Modern—20th century.
NA2335.P75 1999
720'.79—dc21   98–41323

"Matters of Opinion: The Pritzker
Architecture Prize in Historical
Perspective" is copyright © 1999
William J. R. Curtis

Published in 1999 by Harry N. Abrams,
Incorporated, New York

Printed and bound in Japan

Harry N. Abrams, Inc.
100 Fifth Avenue
New York, N.Y. 10011
www.abramsbooks.com

Contents

Foreword

James N. Wood
Director and President, The Art Institute of Chicago

The original idea of creating a major international prize for architecture was first put forth a little more than twenty years ago. With the establishment of an annual award, international in scope and granted to a living architect, Jay and Cindy Pritzker embarked on a path that they hoped would bring increased recognition to the field of architecture and, in turn, enrich public concern for and awareness of the built environment. It was a long-term task, not to be accomplished overnight. It is safe to say, however, that the Pritzker Architecture Prize is today the most prestigious and widely recognized award given to a living architect for a body of work.

The Art Institute of Chicago, at about the same time as the establishment of the Pritzker Architecture Prize, worked toward creating a curatorial Department of Architecture within the museum. The rich heritage of architecture in Chicago and the region and the collection of plans, drawings, sketches, and other documents already housed in the museum's libraries led to the founding of such a department in 1981. That department, the second of its type in an American art museum, has increased its extensive holdings to more than one hundred thousand plans and drawings, including works by the Pritzker laureates, and it annually undertakes a varied program of exhibitions and publications. Perhaps it is a coincidence that these two events, the founding of the prize and the establishment of our architecture department, occurred at roughly the same time, but both symbolize a commitment to the art of architecture, promoting excellence in the field and bringing architecture into the public forum for understanding, debate, and enjoyment.

Chicago is a vibrant city with a long history of outstanding examples of architectural imagination. The history of American architecture could not be written without the names of such great practitioners as Louis Sullivan, Daniel H.

Burnham, Frank Lloyd Wright, Ludwig Mies van der Rohe, and many others. Any reputable survey of world architecture would include these and other Chicago names for contributions made to the fields of architecture, urbanism, and engineering. It would also, undoubtedly, include mention of the Pritzker Architecture Prize, the award established by a Chicago family. It is natural then that the Art Institute should organize an exhibition and publication to honor the Pritzker laureates and view examples of their work. Many of these figures are icons of our time. The twenty-one laureates originating from North America, South America, Europe, and Japan reflect a variety of approaches to the practice of architecture. They all embody excellence in their works, as witnessed by the projects included in this volume.

The Art Institute of Chicago was pleased to host two of the Pritzker award ceremonies, once in 1982 and again in 1988. This book and the exhibition it accompanies represent another, more enduring way to host the Pritzker Architecture Prize again. We thank Jay and Cindy Pritzker and the Hyatt Foundation for making possible a prize that highlights the art of building and for lending their support and encouragement to this project.

A Word from the Chairman of the Jury

J. Carter Brown

It all started with a person I would consider an apt candidate for the *Reader's Digest* "Most Unforgettable Character I Have Met." Carleton Smith conceived the idea of an award to fill in the gap left by the Nobel Prizes, which do not cover the field of architecture. He came to me early on for counsel, as he did with my admired mentor, Kenneth Clark. His first idea was that this architecture prize should be financed by J. Paul Getty.

I remember well our visit to Getty's glorious Elizabethan house, Sutton Place, not far from London. (It is true that the owner had a telephone booth in the front hall so that guests would not be tempted to make long-distance calls at his expense.) I found the owner a curiously sympathetic character, with wide-ranging intellectual interests. However, he was not interested in pursuing Carleton's idea.

It was a characteristic stroke of genius for Carleton to end up with a family whose members have proven to be the ideal patrons of this undertaking. Through their continuing involvement with architecture as *hoteliers* and with their lively interest in all things visual, the Pritzkers have now been identified with the prize to the benefit of both. They have instinctively understood the necessity of an arm's-length relationship with the selection process, so that we on the jury have been left to make determinations on the merits as we see them.

This process is not as easy as it may seem. There is an enormous amount of architectural talent in the world, and it is extremely difficult to justify making distinctions, particularly when so many practitioners work in such divergent styles, and our aim is to reward the individual, not the "ism." (As has been said, "isms" often quickly become "wasms.")

The idea from the beginning has been to hold up exemplars of creative minds that have contributed to the art of architecture. An important criterion is a body of built work. Creative as visionary architects can often be, the full achievement includes his or her ability to carry out a project to serve a purpose, and to have it constructed and paid for as the final realization of that vision. This dimension separates architecture from so many other art forms, which more often have the opportunity to exist for their own sake. At the same time, it gives architecture its unique value to society. Those structures have to stand up; they generally have to keep out the rain; and they need to fulfill a function that has been preordained but is often refined through a symbiotic relationship between architect and client.

Originally we as a jury were concerned that we might run out of superstars as the prize went on year after year. I remember similar discussions as a member of the executive committee of the board of the John F. Kennedy Center for the Performing Arts, which gives the annual Kennedy Center Honors. The talent pool is so impressively large, however, that the problem has turned out to be the opposite: How can we get around to all those who are truly deserving?

We have also been determined that (unlike, for example, the Kennedy Center Honors) not just the nation but the entire world should be our domain. This adds difficulty in searching out talent in parts of the globe that may not have had the financial resources to be active in the commissioning of architecture, and because our jury feels strongly that judgments must ultimately be made on the experience of the work itself, and not simply from photographs. Architectural photography is a separate art form, and the real building is often either better or worse than what one had been led to expect, but rarely exactly the same. Architecture occupies the dimension of time, as well as the other three. One needs to walk through it and feel the progression of spaces; to receive the signals that only one's peripheral vision can provide; and

even to employ other senses, such as hearing, touch, and smell, to experience a work of architecture to the fullest.

The Pritzkers have been sympathetic to the importance of being there, which might differentiate this selection process from those in other fields where jurors can be provided copies of written texts to judge. Our inspection trips have been enormously rewarding, not in the least because the jury tends to talk architecture collegially morning, noon, and night, and all divergent views get a chance to be heard.

Our ultimate feeling about this task is that it is essentially impossible. One cannot entrust absolute judgment to any group of fallible human beings. Very much on our conscience are the brilliant achievements we have not yet been able to reward. However, the cumulative attention that the Pritzker Prize has been able to draw to the art of architecture in general has, we on the jury firmly believe, a great potential ability to benefit society at large. American philosopher Alfred North Whitehead's "habitual contemplation of greatness" is justification for education in so many fields. If this exhibition and publication can carry the good news of architectural excellence into the public consciousness, the brilliance of Carleton Smith's original vision will have been amply confirmed.

Introduction: The Nature of Architecture Prizes

Martha Thorne

The Art Institute of Chicago has chosen this point in the life of the Pritzker Architecture Prize, its twentieth anniversary, to present examples of the work of the laureates, to begin to analyze the impact of the prize on the field of architecture, and to view the evolution of the significance of the prize itself. The authors of this publication write from a variety of vantage points, from very close, as in the case of J. Carter Brown, president of the jury since the inception of the prize, and Bill N. Lacy, the executive director since 1988, to more distant, for historians William J. R. Curtis and Colin Amery. The twenty-one laureates (in 1988 the award was granted to two architects, Oscar Niemeyer and Gordon Bunshaft) are represented by several major buildings and projects each. There are old familiar friends, such as Bunshaft's Lever House, James Stirling's Staatsgalerie extension, or Rafael Moneo's National Museum of Roman Art. There are also very recent projects, such as Renzo Piano's Tjibaou Cultural Center and Robert Venturi's Nikko Resort complex. Although this analysis represents but one point in an ever-evolving process, the bringing together of the laureates and authors fosters the goal of this publication and the exhibition of assessing the significance of the prize and viewing its changing role. It is also an opportunity to honor those who have contributed to shaping architectural history and our built environment at the end of the twentieth century.

The granting of prizes for significant accomplishments in the arts and sciences is not new. Academies have a long tradition of rewarding excellence by inducting outstanding professionals into their ranks and granting awards and medals for special purposes. All professions have honors, awards, and even contests to call attention to distinguished members. Awards have several purposes though, some of which may not even be acknowledged publicly. All of them seek to honor and recognize achievement. They also aim to inspire potential candidates and encourage advancement. They may set standards, either clearly stated or simply implied by the choice and qualifications of the laureates. Certain awards have the additional purpose of linking the grantor and recipient. The good reputation and standard of excellence are somehow shared between the honoree and the grantor, even when there is no real connection between the two. Several prizes have become virtual household names, such as the Nobel Prize, the Pulitzer Prize, and the Academy Awards. These well-known awards signal to the general public what is to be revered and accepted, often without critical analysis.

In some cases the selection procedure rests with a committee of recognized experts. In others the awards are granted by a decision of one's peers. Within the field of architecture, many awards have been established relatively recently. The Pritzker Architecture Prize is but one. When one surveys the prizes, some questions immediately come to mind. How are the decisions made for the granting of prizes? Who sits on the jury? Have the criteria for selection changed or remained the same? When looking more closely at the Pritzker Prize one wonders, Why is it touted as the Nobel Prize of Architecture? Although it does not carry the largest monetary sum of all the architectural prizes, why do members of the profession and journalists so eagerly await the news of who will be named the next winner? To put it simply, where does the Pritzker Architecture Prize fit within the panorama of architectural citations?

Currently there are five major architecture prizes for the body of work of an architect: the Pritzker Prize, the Praemium Imperiale, the Carlsberg Architectural Prize, the RIBA Gold Medal, and the AIA Gold Medal. The first three are private and awarded on behalf of foundations, which represent companies in businesses other than architecture. The last two are awarded by national professional associations – the Royal Institute of British Architects and the American Institute of Architects. In addition to these honors granted to individuals for overall excellence, others do exist that recognize single buildings, certain aspects of a career, or specific concerns of the building process.

The three private awards – the Pritzker, Praemium Imperiale, and Carlsberg – resemble each other in several ways. All are open to any architect, regardless of nationality, location, or focus of work. All three prizes carry a cash award of significance that is not divisible and ranges from $100,000 to $225,000. (The only exception in the history of the Pritzker Prize occurred in 1988, when the two winners split the award.) The RIBA and AIA gold medals carry no cash award. They are seen as the highest recognition of the peer group and have been in existence for a considerably longer time than the private awards.

Although dignitaries often participate in the formal ceremonies to announce and honor the recipients, the Pritzker Prize, Praemium Imperiale, and Carlsberg Prize are not publicly funded, nor are official honors bestowed by a government. American presidents have on two occasions participated in the ceremonies for the awarding of the Pritzker Prize. The Praemium Imperiale is given by the imperial family in Japan. The queen of Denmark presents the Carlsberg. Participation by such notable figures certainly enhances the reputation of the prizes and ensures that they will receive press coverage.

A closer look at the five prominent international citations reveals certain differences in the selection procedures and their objectives. It also points out possible biases inherent in the prizes and assists in understanding how their popular reputations are created.

The Pritzker Architecture Prize was established in 1979 by Jay and Cindy Pritzker and is funded by their family business, the Hyatt Corporation, via a foundation. Its stated purpose is to "honor a living architect whose built work demonstrates a combination of those qualities of talent, vision, and commitment, which produced consistent and significant contributions to humanity and the built environment through the art of architecture." Winners are selected by a jury of about eight people, the composition of which has changed somewhat over the twenty-year life of the prize. It is interesting to note the combination of dynamism and permanence embodied by the jury. Brown has been the chairman since the prize's founding. Ada Louise Huxtable began as a member in 1987. Toshio Nakamura, writer and editor of the prestigious Japanese architectural journal *A+U,* has served for eight years so far. A relative newcomer, since 1996, is architect Jorge Silvetti of Harvard University. Other practicing professionals who have participated in the decision-making process, but for relatively short tenures, are Philip Johnson, Fumihiko Maki (before he won the prize), Frank O. Gehry and Kevin Roche (after they won the prize), and Ricardo Legorreta, Cesar Pelli, and Arata Isozaki (who have not been awarded the prize to date). Continuity is granted by the long-standing members, while the changes in practicing architects ensure that no one trend or slant is continually supported. It also appears that a position on the jury does not guarantee becoming a laureate.

The nomination procedure for the Pritzker Prize is completely open. Any licensed architect may nominate an architect simply by communicating with the executive director of the jury. The executive director actively seeks out nominations from critics, academics, professionals in related fields, and, of course, the jurors. The jury deliberates early in the year. These meetings include visiting many buildings to assess their qualities and determine whether or not they are Pritzker quality. This fieldwork is a particularly positive aspect of the Pritzker and grants strength to the decisions – photographs are poor substitutes for reality when it comes to architecture. The jury reaches a decision in early spring. Usually the official announcement is made in April, and the awards ceremony, with a dinner for several hundred people from the architecture and art communities, takes place in May or June.

The Praemium Imperiale was created in 1988, with the first awards in five artistic categories being granted in October 1989. The official publication of the prize explains that the awards were established to commemorate the one hundredth anniversary of the founding of the Japan Art Association.[1] The declared purpose is to "highlight the role of the arts in achieving understanding among peoples of the world. The prizes are awarded annually to artists chosen from throughout the world . . . [who] make outstanding contributions to the development, promotion, and progress of the arts. [They are] also intended to contribute broadly to the further dissemination of the world's cultural and artistic activities, and to cultivate and encourage future generations of artists."[2] Eligible are all artists of outstanding accomplishment in their field or who are currently engaged in activities with the potential for outstanding results.

There are five categories for the Praemium Imperiale: painting, sculpture, music, theater/film, and architecture. The selection process is a complex, three-tiered system, including nominating committees, a selection committee, and the board of trustees of the Japan Art

Association. At present there are six nominating committees. Each is chaired by an international advisor. The nominating committees consist of ten to fifteen members who meet twice a year. The chairmen, from six different countries, are often former politicians, always people who, according to their brief biographies, have strengthened ties between Japan and other nations. The current chairmen are Umberto Agnelli, the founder of Fiat; Raymond Barre, former prime minister of France and current mayor of Lyon; Edward Heath, former prime minister of the United Kingdom; Yasuhiro Nakasone, former prime minister of Japan; David Rockefeller, Jr., chairman of Rockefeller Financial Services; and Helmut Schmidt, past chancellor of the former West Germany. The advisors gather suggestions from experts in the field in his or her home country (Huxtable, for example, has served on the U.S. advisor's committee). The international advisors then make their recommendations to the selection committee. The advisors can veto the recommendation of the selection committee for a particular field, and have done so. The selection committee is made up of Japanese specialists in each of the five fields; it is chaired by Rokuro Ishikawa for architecture. Once a decision is reached by the selection committee, with the blessing of the advisors, it must be ratified by the board of trustees.

The award includes a cash gift of 15,000,000 yen (in mid-1998 about $105,000). The majority of the expenses related to the prize and its administration is assumed by the Fujisankei Communications Group. As of December 1997 there were eleven additional corporations listed as contributors to an endowment fund to assure the continuity of the prize. The winners are announced at a press conference held in a major city such as London, Rome, Berlin, Paris, or New York. The awards ceremony and commemorative banquet have always taken

place at the Mieji Memorial Hall in Tokyo. In the past several years a reception or luncheon has been given prior to the official ceremony and hosted by heads of state and high-level politicians, among them Queen Elizabeth II and President Bill Clinton and Hillary Rodham Clinton.

In the field of architecture the winners of the Praemium Imperiale have been, in chronological order since 1989, I. M. Pei, Stirling, Gae Aulenti, Gehry, Kenzo Tange, Charles Correa, Piano, Tadao Ando, Richard Meier, and Alvaro Siza. It is interesting to note that all the Praemium Imperiale winners are also Pritzker recipients, with the exception of Correa (who has served on the Pritzker jury since 1993 and is therefore ineligible) and Aulenti (until now, the only woman to be recognized by any of the major private awards). Piano is the only architect to win the Praemium Imperiale (1995) before being selected by the Pritzker jury (1998). Ando won the Pritzker in 1995, the Praemium Imperiale in 1996, and the RIBA Gold Medal in 1997. The trend seems to indicate that, with the exception of Aulenti, the Praemium Imperiale is somewhat conservative in its approach, honoring well-established, previously recognized architects.

The Carlsberg Architectural Prize is a rather young award. Instituted in 1992 by Carlsberg International A/S, the prize was established in recognition of the company's "great appreciation and profound understanding of the importance of fine architecture for the benefit of the general public." The 1998 booklet on the prize states that Carlsberg Brewing Company has always been interested in the pursuit of excellence in architecture.[3] Many pages of the publication list the design awards that various bottling plants and breweries have received. Therefore, it is to be assumed that the architecture prize is a continuation of this tradition.

The prize, sponsored by the New Carlsberg Foundation, the arm of

Carlsberg International that undertakes philanthropic activities, is granted only every three years. The first time around the decision-making process was a two-tiered system, with a selection committee of journalists chaired by Hans Edvard Nørregård-Nielsen, president of the foundation, to identify candidates. The first year a jury of well-known Europeans chose the winner. On all three occasions the selection committee for identifying candidates has been the same: Nørregård-Nielsen acts as chairman of a group heavily weighted in favor of journal editors – François Chaslin of *L'Architecture d'aujourd'hui*, Peter Davey of *The Architectural Review*, and Nakamura of *A+U* (who has also been a member of the Pritzker Prize jury since 1991) – along with Professor Kenneth Frampton of Columbia University and practicing architect Henning Larsen of Copenhagen.

The first year of the prize the selection committee identified seven candidates, from which the jury selected Ando. The jury then was an unlikely mix of business and cultural figures, ranging from the EEC environmental commissioner Carlo Ripa de Meana and Simone Weil, member of the European Parliament, to director/producer Wim Wenders and composer Andrew Lloyd Weber.

The second Carlsberg went to Finnish architect Juha Leiviskä. It seems that this time around the celebrity jury did not convene and the selection committee itself became the jury. From nominations submitted by architectural publications around the world, the new jury selected an architect well established in Finland with a career of more than twenty-five years. He was relatively unknown beyond Scandinavia and certainly not a name heard outside architectural circles. The jury apparently wanted to recognize this more regional approach to architecture over the increasing tendency toward the internationalization of architects and styles. The jury citation commented on

the "great quality of Leiviskä's work, [which] is sensitive to the social context in which it is situated."

In 1998 the same jury of journalists awarded the Carlsberg and its $225,000 purse to Swiss architect Peter Zumthor, who was chosen from a list of twenty-five candidates, among them several Pritzker laureates – Sverre Fehn, Gehry, Moneo, Niemeyer, Piano, and Siza. Once again the jury chose an architect whose buildings display an extremely high level of craftsmanship and sensitivity to context, yet whose oeuvre is relatively small and who is not well known outside the European architectural scene.

The RIBA Gold Medal is granted yearly to "a person or group whose work promoted, either directly or indirectly, the advancement of architecture." Nominations are accepted from any member of the RIBA. The Gold Medal for the promotion of architecture was instituted by Queen Victoria in 1848. The decision-making procedure is undertaken by a jury chosen by the president of the RIBA, and its selection must be ratified by the RIBA council, the organization's governing board. In 1987 the jury included some familiar names: Correa and Huxtable, both of the Pritzker jury, and Frampton, who would later become a Carlsberg juror. The jury for the RIBA Gold can change and does. The 1997 jury that named Ando (the 1995 Pritzker laureate) the winner included three members of the RIBA upper echelon (a past and present president and a president-elect) and six other members – well-known architect Norman Foster; Sir Jack Zunz, an engineer with the large and prestigious Ove Arup partnership; Lord Peter Palumbo, former chair of the Arts Council of Great Britain; architectural writer Dennis Sharp; Sir Colin Stansfield Smith; and Brian Jefferson. In 1998 a jury of seven, which again included the RIBA president and Foster, but with five other different members, recognized Niemeyer with the

Gold Medal. He, like Ando, had already won the Pritzker. The RIBA Gold Medal is an international prize, but as is to be expected, it has favored U.K. and European architects. Only in recent years has the jury casted a wider net for worthy candidates. Of the approximately one hundred fifty winners, only thirteen have been from the United States, three from Japan, one from the former Soviet Union, and one from India. The list of laureates features not only practicing architects but also prominent urbanists, among them Tony Garnier and Sir Raymond Unwin, and great writers and historians, including Sir John Summerson, Sir Nikolas Pevsner, and Colin Rowe. In its more distant history the medal was awarded to Eugène-Émmanuel Viollet-le-Duc (1864), Sir Edwin Lutyens (1921), Frank Lloyd Wright (1941), Le Corbusier (1953), and R. Buckminster Fuller (1968).

In the past twenty years it is more common to find overlap among the prominent architecture prizes. Architects who have received not only the RIBA but also another major international prize are: Stirling, 1980 (Pritzker, 1981; Praemium Imperiale, 1990); Ralph Erskine, 1987 (Wolf Prize [see discussion below], 1983–84); Meier, 1988 (Pritzker, 1984; Praemium Imperiale and AIA Gold, 1997); Piano, 1989 (Pritzker, 1998); Ando, 1997 (Pritzker, 1995; Praemium Imperiale, 1996); and Niemeyer, 1998 (Pritzker, 1980). The RIBA Gold Medal – perhaps because of its age, continuity, and international scope, and despite its imperfections – is still one of the most prestigious and respected prizes, although it clearly represents the establishment from the British perspective.

The American Institute of Architects awards a gold medal as well. Like its counterpart, the RIBA Gold, this honor carries no monetary compensation. It was established in 1907 and is granted "when appropriate." The Gold Medal, presented to an individual, and the AIA Architecture Firm Award are the highest honors

that the organization confers. Revisions were recently made to the selection process in order to provide the national board of directors with greater exposure to potential candidates and to encourage broader participation in the nominating process. An advisory jury was established to help guide the board in choosing a winner. The advisory jury must include, but is not limited to, a board member, a former gold medalist, and one member of each of the AIA's committees on design, education, and practice management. Nominations are made via the committees or board members. The advisory jury then selects five of the nominees to be forwarded to the board. Additional graphic documentation and information are submitted, and the board then makes its final decision.

Fifty-five medals have been awarded since the institution of the AIA Gold in 1907. Recipients include Charles McKim of McKim, Mead, and White (1909), Louis Sullivan (1944), Wright (1949), Ludwig Mies van der Rohe (1960), Le Corbusier (1961), and Louis Kahn (1971). Not all winners were selected without controversy. In surveying the history of the medal, one sees that public opinion and image have been factors in the deliberations. Wright's name was proposed year after year, yet he was not a member of the AIA and had even publicly criticized the organization and its members. However, by 1949 Wright could not be neglected any longer, especially after having been recognized by the RIBA in 1941. Finally, after much heated debate among the board members, even to the point of questioning Wright's professional and private morals, the decision was reached to bestow the medal on one of the truly outstanding figures of American architecture. This episode served to call into question the conservative tradition of the award.

In the recent past the AIA Gold Medal has been bestowed almost exclusively on American architects. Since 1967 the only non-Americans to win have been one Canadian (Arthur Erickson, 1989) and one Englishman (Foster, 1994), although earlier Alvar Aalto and Pier Luigi Nervi, among a few others, were honored. Three architects received the AIA Gold and then the Pritzker: Tange, Johnson, and Pei. Two received the Pritzker and then the AIA Gold: Roche and Meier. This seems to indicate that if one is American and a Pritzker Prize winner, one also has a good chance at an AIA Gold Medal.

Another honor granted by a community of peers is membership in the American Academy of Arts and Letters. This organization was established in 1904 as a subgroup of the one-hundred-fifty-member National Institute of Arts and Letters, which had been formed six years earlier. It was thought that a more select association, chosen from the members of the institute, might infuse the parent organization with needed energy, funds, and prestige. Initially the academy had thirty members; this number was increased to fifty in 1907. The academy's early constitution provided that it would be a cultural advisor to the government and to the general public and would stimulate activity in the arts through the granting of prizes. In 1971 the academy and the institute began proceedings to merge again into a single organization, and today it is known as the American Academy of Arts and Letters. Membership in the academy is one type of award. Additionally, many committees within the Institute–Academy have distributed prizes, such as the Arnold W. Brunner Award in Architecture.

Even during its early years, there was a concern about the East Coast bias of the academy. Vocal opposition by some members of Congress in response to the bill brought before it in 1909 to establish the academy's national charter complained about the lack of members from many states. The membership lists reveal that this trend is evident throughout the organization's history. Recent president (and

Pritzker Prize winner) Roche addressed the issue of biases in the membership roster and in 1995 suggested that, "In proposing candidates for membership, you [the members] may wish to consider broadening the selection to include a better geographic, ethnic, and gender representation of our society . . . it is suggested to look beyond the usual circle of acquaintances on the East Coast for worthy candidates. . . . More than half the entire membership lives in Connecticut, New Jersey, and New York. . . . Only one sixth of the membership are women. There are six African-American members and two Asian-American members."[4]

The academy members include all the American Pritzker Prize winners. All were invited to join before they were awarded the Pritzker: Bunshaft was elected to the Institute–Academy in 1960 and received the Pritzker in 1988; Johnson, 1963 and 1979, respectively; Pei, 1963 and 1983; Roche, 1970 and 1982; Meier, 1983 and 1984; Gehry, 1987 and 1989; and Venturi, 1990 and 1991. Honorary foreign members also include several Pritzker laureates: Stirling and Aldo Rossi were elected to the academy after becoming Pritzker laureates, and Niemeyer and Tange were inducted before winning the Pritzker. Current foreign architects who belong to the academy but have not won the Pritzker are few: Correa and Isozaki.

Numerous other prizes and honorary affiliations provide the means to recognize architects, firms, and buildings. Specific requirements, purposes, and procedures may vary, but all seek to identify and celebrate achievement as defined by the granting board or institution.

For example, the Aga Khan Award for Architecture recognizes only projects that have been completed for at least two years. The award was established in 1977 by Prince Karim Aga Khan and first granted in 1980, just one year after the first Pritzker Architecture Prize was conferred. In the mid-1970s the rise in oil prices fueled new construction booms; it was also a time of redefinition of the Muslim world vis-à-vis the Western world. These factors, and undoubtedly many others, gave rise to the Aga Khan Award along with an architectural journal, symposia, workshops, and programs at Harvard and MIT on Islamic architecture. The award's stated goals are "to encourage an understanding and awareness of the strength and diversity of Muslim cultural traditions, which, when combined with an enlightened use of modern technology, . . .will result in buildings more appropriate for the Islamic world of tomorrow."[5] Despite the fact that diverse styles, approaches, and types are considered, the clearly defined focus of "works for the Muslim world" limits the scope and reduces the field of possible candidates. Works in all countries are considered, but those in Muslim countries are of greatest interest to the "master jury." The distinct makeup of each jury, which changes with every cycle of the prize, and a dynamic cultural scene have contributed to marked shifts in the kinds of buildings cited and the criteria established for judging the nominated works.

For the Aga Khan Award, as for the Praemium Imperiale, the determination process is complicated. Nominations are solicited for realized works of architecture and urban design. They are then evaluated by a steering committee and technical experts, who visit the sites. Finally the master jury of world-renowned architects and scholars decides which works will be cited for the triennial awards and which firms will share the approximately $500,000 in prize money. Jury members have included Gehry, Hans Hollein, Tange, Stirling, Peter Eisenman, Maki, and Balkrishna Doshi. To date, after six cycles of the prize, more than seventy projects have been singled out for the Aga Khan Award from a pool of more than one thousand six hundred nominations.

The Aga Khan Award for Architecture has a second means of celebrating individuals that resembles other privately funded prizes honoring an entire career: the Chairman's Award. On two occasions the Chairman's Award has been bestowed on an architect who has "made a lifelong contribution and commitment to architecture in the Muslim world": Hassan Fathy in 1980 and Rifat Chadirji in 1986. To date there has been no overlap between the Pritzker Architecture Prize and the Aga Khan Chairman's Award. Although both honor long-term achievement, the framework that defines each is very different.

The Wolf Prizes in the Arts are awarded with the same aim as those in sciences: to honor achievements that benefit mankind. The Wolf Foundation was established in 1975 with an endowment of $1,000,000 by Israeli chemist Dr. Ricardo Wolf and his wife. Wolf, who immigrated to Cuba before World War I, served as ambassador to Israel, where he remained with his wife even after President Fidel Castro severed diplomatic ties with Israel in 1973, until his death in 1981. The awards carry a gift of $100,000 for each of the fields of medicine, agriculture, chemistry, physics, and the arts – a category that includes architecture along with painting, music, and sculpture, and thus translates into an award to an architect or architects once every four years. Winners are chosen from candidates submitted by deans and directors of colleges and schools of architecture, and directors of professional associations throughout the world. The names of the jury members – three experts, one each from the U.S., Europe, and Israel – are not revealed. Only their final decision is announced. The winners to date have been Erskine (1983–84), Maki and Giancarlo de Carlo (1988), Gehry, Jørn Utzon, and Sir Denys Lasdun (1992), and Frei Otto and Aldo van Eyck (1996–97). The jury citations consistently comment on the social value of the art.

Because it is frequently shared, the Wolf award may not carry the cachet of the Pritzker or other prizes that are granted to just one professional; however, the choices to date have been unique. Maki and Gehry were the only two who had previously won the Pritzker and could be considered part of the international star system of architects. The other winners are all solid professionals, though perhaps less well known to the general public, and all are practicing architects. The choices seem to indicate support for the craft of building.

Other prizes include the more recently created UIA Gold Medal, awarded by the Union Internationale des Architectes (International Union of Architects). The UIA, based in Paris, is a worldwide alliance of national professional associations of architecture. It seems to be a sort of United Nations of the field, and one wonders if diplomatic concerns influence the jury's decisions. The Gold Medal is granted triennially to an architect for an outstanding career. The jury of the UIA award is composed of the organization's president along with five other representatives, and together they seek to identify an architect who has made a "lifetime contribution to the improvement of the quality of life for society and the architectural profession." The medal was first given in 1984 to Fathy. The committee cited his "pursuit of cultural significance that has not only provided lessons from the old and traditional, but has emphasized the spiritual qualities [of architecture]." Reima Pietilä of Finland won the medal in 1987, Correa in 1990, Maki in 1993, and Moneo in 1996, just months after receiving the Pritzker Prize.

In 1994 Gehry became the first recipient of the Dorothy and Lillian Gish Award for lifetime contribution to the arts. This is a striking accomplishment because the prize is not just for architecture but all the arts. The $250,000 award is granted annually to a "man or woman who has made an outstanding contribu-

tion to the beauty of the world." The jury for the Gish Award included only one architect, Hugh Hardy of Hardy Holzman Pfeiffer Associates of New York, along with actress Carol Burnett, actor Roddy McDowall, and musician John Williams.

There are numerous honors for buildings, such as the Stirling Prize for Architecture, sponsored by the London *Sunday Times* and the RIBA for the best new British-designed building; it includes a cash prize of $32,000. Since 1988 the Mies van der Rohe Foundation has administered a process that annually identifies high-quality recent buildings in the European Economic Community. The AIA grants a twenty-five-year award to an outstanding building in the U.S. between twenty-five and thirty-five years old that exemplifies design of enduring significance. There are also hundreds of prizes given by every sector of the building industry to promote their own special causes – stone, brick, glass, aluminum, and so on.

With so many prizes being given for apparently similar purposes, do they still have a value? Of course, certain commendable functions are fulfilled by the granting of prizes. The debate and attention focused on the built environment is at an all-time high. Although not as widely covered in the general press as other artistic fields, architecture has made enormous strides in past years in this direction. Time, however, is the true test of a prize. The more open, consistent, and coherent the selection criteria and the longer the prize exists, the more prestigious the award. On these fronts the Pritzker Architecture Prize leads the group of privately funded awards. The Pritzker family began the award at a time when Americans' appreciation of architecture was just beginning to extend beyond national boundaries. Today international commissions are the norm, and it is not uncommon for a city or town to desire a "signature" building. To have founded a prize in 1979 and to continue supporting it today is positive in and of itself.

It must also be recognized that the marketing efforts of the Pritzker Prize are significant. A publication on the laureate is produced each year and widely distributed to the press, libraries, art and architecture organizations, and individuals. The Pritzker Prize is the first to have its own web site. An annual dinner for up to five hundred people held in a different city each year at an architecturally significant site contributes to the prestige and ceremony surrounding the award.

The open nominations procedure and the independence of the jury are two aspects that support calling the prize the Nobel of architecture. The composition of the jury, which is relatively small and basically stable, has led to a remarkably consistent high standard in the selection of laureates. The jury members come from several countries. They are not exclusively architectural critics or practicing architects. The deliberations are direct and the jury alone makes the decision. The Pritzker jury is more a collection of individuals rather than representatives of other concerns.

The true test of the Pritzker Prize, however, is yet to come. For it to remain in the forefront it must not simply echo choices made in other arenas. The jury will probably continue its natural evolution, welcoming new participants as current members step down. The delicate balance of personalities, countries, professions, and concerns should be maintained. The jury's future choices and the message these selections communicate are crucial. One hopes that the jury will continue to seek out excellence, not trends. It should broaden its field when considering possible candidates, and continue to step beyond what is famous in favor of quality. No woman has as yet won the Pritzker, a disturbing fact that reveals much about the traditional structure of the profession and the deficiencies of reward systems. Although many of the winners are at a mature point in their career when they are recognized, some are honored not only for works completed but for the potential of projects yet to be realized. Future Pritzker juries must be bold enough to make the prize even more one of recognition of a career in progress, not a stamp of approval given in retrospect.

Notes

1   Japan Art Association, *Praemium Imperiale 1997* (Tokyo: Japan Art Association, 1997).

2   Ibid., p. 15.

3   Carlsberg International A/S, *Carlsberg Architectural Prize* (Copenhagen: Carlsberg International A/S, 1998).

4   Hortense Calisher, "1988–1997: Decade of Reunion," in John Updike, ed., *A Century of Arts and Letters* (New York: Columbia University Press, 1998), p. 290.

5   Azim A. Nanji, ed., *Building for Tomorrow: The Aga Khan Award for Architecture* (London: Academy, 1994), p. 98.

The Pritzker Architecture Prize: The First Twenty Years

Bill N. Lacy

Throughout history it has been important for civilizations both to do great deeds and to honor their doing. The impulse to acknowledge extraordinary individual achievements has been an essential part of every society large and small, from identifying the high school valedictorian to decorating the war hero, from awarding Boy Scout merit badges to conferring the Nobel Prize. The college diploma is given added value by designating a select number of them summa cum laude degrees. Prizes are not simply a means to reward but also a way to set high standards and reaffirm the importance of having such criteria for human endeavors.

In this spirit the Pritzker Architecture Prize was established in 1979 to assure that architecture, one of our most ubiquitous art forms and one that is an unavoidable presence in our lives, would receive the level of public awareness it deserved. It was felt that such a goal could best be accomplished by awarding an annual prize to one of the leading practitioners of this hybrid profession – the most scientific of the arts and the most artistic of the sciences. The architect so honored should have "produced consistent and significant contributions to humanity and the built environment through the art of architecture." Guidelines laid down at the outset were that the prize would be international in scope and given to a living architect for a body of built work. The prize consisted of a $100,000 cash award, a citation, and until 1987 a limited-edition Henry Moore sculpture, replaced in subsequent years with a bronze medallion. To further highlight the purpose of the prize and bring greater attention to the laureate, we have selected architecturally significant sites around the world in which to hold the awards ceremony. They have included numerous leading museums in the United States and Europe, the Todai-ji Buddhist temple in Nara, Japan, the Grand Trianon and the Palace of Versailles, and Prague Castle.

In 1978, when the Pritzker Architecture Prize was conceived as a strategy for honoring a profession whose members were often overlooked, even at dedication ceremonies of buildings they had designed, it was regarded as an original and unprecedented idea. The anonymity of architecture and the general public's lack of awareness of its influence on their lives was a condition of the times. The notion that buildings and the spaces they create, places where people work, live, shop, and worship, could have any real influence on one's life and behavior was not a part of the collective public consciousness. Even the appearance of Philip Johnson, the first Pritzker Prize winner, on the cover of *Time* magazine did little to raise the recognition of the architect's place in contemporary society. Ayn Rand's *The Fountainhead* and Gary Cooper had done more.

In the years since the founding of the prize, architecture has enjoyed an ever-growing popularity and global visibility, with a proliferation of publications, the appointment of architecture critics at major newspapers, popular TV shows, and a greater appreciation of our cultural heritage and the need to preserve historic buildings and districts. We have witnessed the rise of the architect from obscurity to superstardom; we have seen architecture become a recognized and valued commodity in the world of commercial and cultural competitiveness, watched it cross the threshold from meager commissions to megaprojects whose gigantism reduces the human scale to Lilliputian dimensions. Architecture has firmly entered the realm of public debate and social conversation as a topic of importance and late-night talk shows.

Proof that the Pritzker Prize's early goal of gaining greater visibility for architects and architecture was provided in dramatic fashion on the occasion of the twentieth anniversary of the prize, when the awards dinner was held at the White House. There, five hundred architects, guests, patrons, clients, and others interested in architecture gathered to honor that year's recipient. In 1979 it was difficult to persuade the president of the United States to mention in a speech the phrase "quality of life" as it related to the built environment, much less the word "architecture." But on this anniversary occasion, Bill Clinton said to the assembled audience under a billowing white tent on the South Lawn, "Our buildings, our monuments embody our frontier spirit, our exuberance, our optimism, our determination. In honoring the past you can help us imagine the future. All of you – by nature, instinct, training, and will – are builders. The country and the world need its builders, those with imagination and hope and heart." He quoted Frank Lloyd Wright as saying that "every great architect is necessarily a poet" and stated that an architect "must be a great original interpreter of his time," acknowledging that the twenty-first laureate, Renzo Piano, was such a person.

At the heart of the Pritzker Architecture Prize, and the success it has enjoyed, is the jury who selects the winning architect each year. During the past two decades the jury's composition has gradually changed, but with few exceptions it has been consistent in its purpose and procedures. Its international members have maneuvered their way through an ever-evolving scene of architectural theories, manifestos, cliques, fashionable trends, and shifting economic, political, and social circumstances, each year selecting a person whose work embodies characteristics they find admirable, enduring, and deserving of recognition in a long tradition that dates back to the pyramids and ancient Greece.

When Jay and Cindy Pritzker established the prize they used good judgment in agreeing on flexible guidelines, a selection process that was not unduly complex or bureaucratic in nature, and a jury of superior qualifications, which would do the choosing. The Pritzkers do not participate

Christoph, son of Carleton Smith, Philip Johnson, Cindy Pritzker, and President Jimmy Carter at the 1979 award presentation at Dumbarton Oaks, Washington, D.C.

President Bill Clinton, First Lady Hillary Rodham Clinton, Cindy and Jay Pritzker, Emilia Rossato Piano, and Renzo Piano at the 1998 award presentation at the White House

Gottfried Böhm, the 1986 laureate, and Jay Pritzker at Goldsmiths' Hall, London, England

in either the solicitation of nominations for the prize or in the selection. They are, however, keenly interested and involved in all other aspects of the calendar of yearly events associated with the awarding of the prize.

Those who are asked to serve on the jury are chosen with particular care – individuals noted for their broad international experience and knowledge of the field, fair and unbiased judgment, professional integrity, and a passion for architecture and the arts. Another more personal factor also comes into play in the choice of a new jury member. The Pritzkers are a family known for their closeness and they have over the years picked jury members with great care and thoughtfulness, knowing that these people will unavoidably become a part of their extended family. The degree to which the Pritzkers allow the jury to operate without patronly interference, and a measure of their trust, is exemplified by the fact that they do not even know, each year, which architects are under consideration or who has been selected until the executive director informs them of the decision immediately following the jury meeting.

The appointment of J. Carter Brown as chairman of the first jury was a natural choice, and he has served with judicious distinction in that capacity for the entirety of the prize's existence. For many years Mr. Brown served as director of the National Gallery of Art in Washington, D.C., and he continues to act as chairman of the United States Fine Arts Commission. He is a fierce defender of the nation's patrimony, an advisor to presidents on cultural matters, and limitlessly well versed on the subject of architecture.

The next member recruited for the founding jury was the distinguished and esteemed historian of art and architecture, and host of the very popular BBC television series "Civilization," the late Kenneth Clark (Lord Clark of Saltwood). The other three members of the first jury, who

set the ongoing standard of excellence for the prize, were J. Irwin Miller, chairman of Cummins Engine Company, patron of the arts and architecture, and the inventor of the widely hailed strategy to make midwestern Columbus, Indiana, an unequaled showcase of contemporary architecture in small-town America; Cesar Pelli, noted architect and dean, at the time, of the prestigious Yale University School of Architecture; and Arata Isozaki, a prominent Japanese architect.

How does the jury go about its work? The Pritzker Prize selection process is simple and straightforward. Nominations are open to all licensed architects, but each year the executive director is charged with soliciting nominations from a global network of knowledgeable persons in the profession. Additional recommendations are gathered from past and present jury members as well as all the Pritzker Prize winners. Materials and qualifications are assembled on a number of architects to be presented to the jury each year for their consideration in a two-day session. The Pritzker Architecture Prize is a competition, but an unusual one. An architect may enter the competition by self-nomination, as you will see from the story that follows, but that is rare and in general a nominee is not aware that he or she is being considered. The winner does not receive a commission to build, only the recognition that he or she has reached one of the highest levels of distinction in the field of architecture. The proof that any qualified person can apply occurred in 1989, when I received a call from an anonymous gentleman:

"How do I nominate someone for the Pritzker Architecture Prize?" he asked.

"You tell me his or her name," I said.

"That's it? You don't have to fill out forms, list accomplishments, submit a portfolio and letters of references? You don't have to be recommended?" he asked incredulously.

"No, just tell me the name, and I'll do the rest," I said. "If the person is eligible for consideration, I will gather the material and present it to the jury for consideration."

A pause.

"Then I would like to recommend myself."

"And your name, sir?" I asked.

"I am Gordon Bunshaft," he replied.

"Thank you, Mr. Bunshaft."

That was the year Gordon Bunshaft won the prize, sharing it with Oscar Niemeyer.

One of the reasons the jury can operate in the fashion that it does, without the encumbrance of voluminous dossiers and research materials to justify the awarding of the prize, is its premise that the buildings are the proof of each candidate's qualifications, not publications, not books, not slide presentations or other awards. No Pritzker Prize is ever awarded without the jury's seeing a substantial number of buildings by the architect. This is why the site visits are an essential element of the process, and they are augmented by the travel that each of the jury members pursues in the normal course of his or her professional activities each year. Whereas slides are the usual currency of groups charged with selecting architects for commissions or prizes, in the case of the Pritzker jury, they serve simply as an aide-mémoire. The following are some notes I made on one of the jury's recent trips.

February 1998
We were traveling to Venice to meet and select the twenty-first Pritzker Architecture Prize winner. The sleek white private Canadair jet with "N831CJ" neatly lettered on the tail ("CJ" for Cindy and Jay Pritzker) was parked in its place at the Marine Air Terminal at LaGuardia at 7:00 A.M. as scheduled.

Members of the jury were assembled in the small waiting room of the private anteroom of the larger Delta Air Shuttle operation: J. Carter Brown, the longtime chairman and director emeritus of the National Gallery of Art; Jorge Silvetti, head of Harvard's architecture program and partner in the Boston firm of Machado and Silvetti; Toshio Nakamura, former editor of the Japanese magazine *A+U*, now with the Japan Institute of Architects; and Ada Louise Huxtable, author and noted doyenne of architectural criticism, critic at the *New York Times* for many years and most recently at the *Wall Street Journal*; and myself. We were five in number. We would be joined at our destination in Venice later that evening by Charles Correa, a much-honored architect from Bombay, and on the following day by Giovanni Agnelli, the senior corporate leader of Italy's Fiat empire and a member of the jury. Lord Jacob Rothschild had been excused due to pressing Heritage Fund business in London. Sr. Agnelli was hosting our jury meeting at the Palazzo Grassi, and our visit was fortunately timed to coincide with the opening of a major Picasso show there.

It was a mild and sunny day. A van took us to the plane, and we climbed up the steps to meet a crew now familiar to us from previous excursions. There were seating accommodations for ten, but we rarely had more than six on any of our trips.

This was not a plane full of passengers who read or slept very much or watched in-flight movies. It was a group who enjoyed each other's company and had come to accept and be amused by personal foibles, habits, and eccentricities, and who had enormous respect for the judgment, integrity, professional experience, and knowledge of one another. From the moment we assembled, a non-stop marathon discussion of architecture began, on the way to and from the plane, in the plane, touring the various buildings. It was incessant and unstoppable.

Thomas Pritzker, Bill N. Lacy, Jay Pritzker, Frank O. Gehry, J. Carter Brown, and Kenzo Tange at the Todai-ji Buddhist temple, Nara, Japan, in 1989

It was also exhausting because the passion for architecture was never sated. Only when we slept and were separated did the avalanche of words and ideas cease; it would be triggered again over breakfast or on the way to the airport the next morning.

On this particular trip we would cover eleven countries and seven cities in nine days. We would ride in numerous vehicles to see two dozen buildings by architects from Italy, Switzerland, the U.S.A., Finland, Spain, and the Netherlands. This demanding tour would include a dramatic snowstorm in Helsinki, a riotous celebration of Carnevale in Basel, motorboat rides on the canals of Venice and Amsterdam to approach key buildings from the water, and side trips to spectacular classics such as the restored Chiesa dei Miracoli in Venice and in the Netherlands the famous Schröder House by Rietveld, a masterful city hall by Dudok, and the Educatorium by Rem Koolhaas.

As Ada Louise Huxtable said succinctly of the necessity of such an approach, "We go to see the buildings because the buildings can't come to see us."

As compelling and seductive as photographs of buildings are, the buildings themselves in their context and spatial reality are the primary basis on which the prize is awarded each year. Photographic representations of architecture are always misleading, since they represent only two dimensions of a three-dimensional art form. The site visits allow the jury to follow the work of architects who are perennially under consideration, as well as that of promising younger architects. Portions of the itinerary are also sometimes devoted to a trend or movement in a particular part of the world, and afford the jury the opportunity to test its current attitudes about architecture by visiting milestone buildings by past masters.

It must be an odd sight to the passerby to see the jury members arrive at a building for viewing, descend from a black van, fan out around the target with cameras blazing, like some architectural SWAT team, and study details with the intensity reserved for detectives looking for fingerprints or other clues, all the while carrying on conversations rich with observations about plan and section, sources of light, unexpected juxtapositions of volumes, views within and without, and inevitably, comparisons with other buildings, current and historical. In these visual and verbal assaults on selected buildings, the jury is constantly searching for work that is original without being clever, that adheres to age-old principles of architecture but is not predictable; buildings whose concept is readily revealed and whose details add to that premise in a hierarchical way. The making of architecture is a complex and difficult undertaking, and the jury must take into account the thousands of design decisions, including political and economic constraints, that were made to realize each building it views.

The profession of architecture is aligned with a tradition of creating monuments and lesser structures that stretches back to the beginning of history. Buildings from the ancient world still exist. Although many of the architects' names remain a mystery, the evidence of their designs is the most lasting record we have of civilizations past, and the buildings are readily accessible in a way that other historical evidence is not. It may be presumptuous of us to have a Pritzker Architecture Prize, to single out architects for designs executed in only a relative speck of time. But the work the prize has honored represents an essential chapter in architectural history, and shows where we as a culture were at this brief moment in time.

Admittedly, there are shortcomings to be pointed out. No woman has yet been awarded the prize. And although our intentions are to be international in scope, so far the winners have all been drawn from the United States, western Europe, and Japan. We have not moved apprecia-

Guests at the 1992 dinner at the Harold Washington Library, Chicago, Illinois, honoring Alvaro Siza

bly from honoring architects whose body of work consists primarily of individual bravura buildings and commercial structures to lauding those engaged in public-housing projects, for example. There is a disappointing lack of winners from developing countries, where sophisticated building technology is rare and the execution of award-winning designs is therefore hindered. We have these issues and many more to address in the next twenty years.

As Colin Amery says at the beginning of his essay, "Giving prizes away is not easy." It is not easy, but it is extremely rewarding both to the giver and the receiver. The Pritzker Architecture Prize has filled a void in the awareness of the art of architecture by singling out some of the most talented and committed practitioners of our time, by calling public attention to one of the oldest activities of humankind – one that combines utilitarian and aesthetic purposes – and by affirming, through its choices, the prize's credo of "Firmness, Commodity, and Delight" in architecture.

to cross boundaries between the various arts. As the author of many books on architecture, he was also deeply involved in preserving the best of New York City's many fine buildings.

The late Arthur Drexler, director of the Department of Architecture and Design at The Museum of Modern Art, New York, played a key role as consultant to the jury in its first decade, along with Stuart Wrede, who succeeded him.

Managing the prize's organization, jury meetings, and logistical details would not have been possible without the valued services of my longtime colleague, Lita Talarico.

And finally, during my tenure, Keith Walker and his partner Robert Jensen have been responsible for myriad press and public relations activities associated with the prize as well as publications, exhibitions, televised seminars, and, most important, the annual ceremonies at which the prize is awarded. They have been critical in assuring that the Pritzker Prize receives widespread attention each year.

Note

In addition to the Pritzkers and the jurors, who deserve congratulations for this twenty-year experiment and its success, there are many others who have played seminal roles in the prize. In particular, I would like to single out the contribution of my two predecessors in the role of secretary to the jury (later changed to executive director). It was the late Carleton Smith, an indescribable entrepreneur who seemed part royal family and part P. T. Barnum, who put all this in motion, set the style of the prize, and understood its importance from the beginning.

Possibly only one individual could have followed Carleton and operated with the same theatrical flair, the late Brendan Gill. Brendan was widely hailed for his broad range of interests, which included architecture along with literature, film, and theater. He was identified for many years with the *New Yorker* magazine as a critic with a cultural passport that allowed him

The 1997 prize was awarded to Sverre Fehn at the Guggenheim Museum in Bilbao, Spain

Matters of Opinion:
The Pritzker Architecture Prize
in Historical Perspective

William J. R. Curtis

Twenty years is a long time in the history of a prize but a short time in the history of architecture. With the millennium approaching, and with the Pritzker Architecture Prize celebrating two decades of its existence, this may be a good moment to look back over several of the annual selections and to consider them in a historical perspective. Architectural fashions come and go, but durable buildings remain. In fact they settle into history in unexpected ways. With a little distance, long-term patterns begin to emerge.

The first Pritzker laureate was Philip Johnson (1979); the most recent, Renzo Piano (1998). A survey of all the names in between reveals a wide range of buildings, positions, personalities, and cultures.[1] There is no obvious tendency in these selections beyond some vague intention of picking "the best," and there is no particular party line. Had there been an attempt at imposing an exclusive ideological position, it would probably have been overtaken by the unpredictability of artistic creation: architects and works of real interest refuse to fit a priori categories and demand to be experienced and judged with a fresh eye.

The Pritzker Prize has honored some of the key figures of recent world architecture, for example, Frank O. Gehry (1989), Alvaro Siza (1992), and Tadao Ando (1995). But the jury has usually waited until an architect's reputation was firmly established before bestowing the award. It has not assigned itself a pathfinding role in the identification of young talent and emerging ideas. In fact the Pritzker Prize has sometimes had a restorative function, reinstating senior citizens from the history of modern architecture and giving them a recognition denied them in their time.

The last twenty years in architecture have been characterized by pluralism. If anything, this has made the task of the Pritzker juries easier as it has allowed for the recognition of quality in diverse forms. While there has evidently been a response to the changing aims of the discipline, the choices have rarely been conditioned directly by shifts in contemporary opinion. The juries themselves have altered over the years, and the selection process is too complex to obey any single point of view. Moreover, it is the entire oeuvre of an architect that is taken into account. In some cases, such as Kenzo Tange, Luis Barragán, or Sverre Fehn, this has meant looking back to works created three or four decades before.

While some decisions have been rather too obvious in their designation of accredited (and often overrated) "stars," others have been courageous departures from what was in vogue. To have chosen the Mexican architect Barragán in 1980 required some independence from the fashions and slogans of the moment, especially as most of his major works had been realized in the 1940s and 1950s. The choice of Oscar Niemeyer, the Brazilian modernist whose masterpiece, the Casino at Pampulha, Belo Horizonte, in Minas Gerais, Brazil (1940–43), preceded his selection by almost half a century, also necessitated a degree of historical maturity and cultural latitude. He shared the 1988 Pritzker with Gordon Bunshaft,

Luis Barragán. Egerstrom House and San Cristóbal Stables, Los Clubes, Atizapán de Zaragoza, Mexico City. 1967–68

author of at least two key twentieth-century skyscrapers – Lever House, New York (1951–52), and the National Commercial Bank in Jeddah, Saudi Arabia (1977–83) – but a figure completely out of step with the critical prejudices prevalent in the late 1980s.

Not that the Pritzker laureates have always matched up to the myth of "Nobel Prize–winners in Architecture." Whatever his capacities to respond to urban contexts, the German architect Gottfried Böhm (1986) hardly emerges as a figure of international, let alone universal, significance. Christian de Portzamparc (1994) was also a surprising choice for many, his detractors claiming that he was a superficial neo-Corbusian mannerist, his supporters arguing that he was researching new spatial concepts for the postindustrial city. The recent selection of the Norwegian Fehn (1997) has also been the occasion for polemics, one of the strangest objections being that he was not well enough known![2] In fact it is precisely the modesty and silent presence of Fehn's architecture that probably recommended him to the jury, especially at a time of overwhelming rhetorical noise in the theorizing around architecture.

History is liable to look askance at some of the omissions as well as some of the selections. Given the unevenness of quality among the laureates (and even within their respective oeuvres) it is altogether puzzling that the Danish architect Jørn Utzon, born in 1918, the designer of the magisterial Sydney Opera House (1957–73) and the Church at Bagsvaerd near Copenhagen (1969–76), has not received the recognition he deserves. Had the jury cast its critical net wider it might have pulled up other architects of a high order, such as the Spanish architect Alejandro de la Sota, who died two years ago at the age of eighty-two. His Civil Government Building in Tarragona (1954–57) and his Maravillas School Gymnasium in Madrid (1961–62) stand out in retrospect as buildings timeless but of their time.

Gordon Bunshaft with Skidmore, Owings, and Merrill. National Commercial Bank, Jeddah, Saudi Arabia. 1977–83

These reticent and enigmatic works have been seminal for several later generations of Spanish architects; but they also take their place in the general history of twentieth-century architecture.

No doubt there are other names that one could add to the list (the British architects Denys Lasdun and Norman Foster both come to mind), but the intention here is rather to review the selections so far made. With well-endowed international prizes there will always be squabbles over who is the most deserving and who has been left out. In the end a certain durable quality is what counts, and this implies a capacity to transcend contemporary trends and to maintain a historical perspective by keeping an eye on past works of excellence, while recognizing that which is fresh and vital. The most radical innovations have a way of opening up new expressive territories, even as they return to certain core values in the art of architecture.

Over the twenty years preceding the founding of the prize in 1979, the originating modern masters – figures like Frank Lloyd Wright, Le Corbusier, Ludwig Mies van der Rohe, and Alvar Aalto – disappeared from the world scene; in the 1970s architects of the stature of Louis Kahn and Carlo Scarpa also died. These were hard acts to follow. In the polemics of postmodernism in the early 1980s, as much as possible was done to forget this powerful heritage. In an atmosphere of turbulent transition and enforced amnesia, exaggerated claims were made on all sides. This did not make the task of sensible criticism any easier.[3]

The Pritzker Prize emerged at a time of questioning in which there was much vocal skepticism about the tenets (or what were thought to have been the tenets) of earlier "modernism." But rhetorical declarations are one thing, forms another, and the "substructures" of modern architecture simply refused to go away. The majority of the Pritzker winners were born between 1905 and 1935 and were therefore (willingly or unwillingly) heirs to a diverse modern tradition. Most of them defined their respective positions during the three decades after World War II in response to the contradictory cultural currents of the time, but also through a critical transformation of preceding architectural ideas.[4]

In this respect it is interesting to contrast the work of the first two Pritzker laureates, Johnson and Barragán, both born in the first decade of this century. The brochure that accompanied Johnson's award showed a selection of competent but unexceptional work, most of which was safely within the modern architectural pale, from the Glass House in New Canaan, Connecticut (1947–49), up to the then recently completed Garden Grove Community Church, California (1977–80). The notorious AT&T skyscraper in New York (1979–84), with its Chippendale top and various other historical allusions, which contributed to the postmodernist tendency of making superficial quotations, had not yet been unveiled. One should not forget that Johnson had always been interested in a form of stripped neoclassicism, even within the obvious neo-Miesian language of the Glass House. At times this resulted in devalued expressions, such as the stilted monumentality of the New York State Theater at Lincoln Center (1958–64). In his acceptance address Johnson made reference to a grand pedigree: "Here in the West we are blessed with a great artistic heritage – in this century alone we have Frank Lloyd Wright, Le Corbusier, Lutyens, Mies van der Rohe. . . ."[5]

The skeptics looked upon the selection of Johnson as evidence that the new award was already in the hands of that nebulous entity, "the New York cultural elite." It seemed an unlikely choice if the aim was to announce a prize recognizing world-quality architecture. The situation was saved (somewhat) by the choice the following year of Barragán, though it should not be forgotten that he had recently gone through the local accreditation process of a show at The Museum of

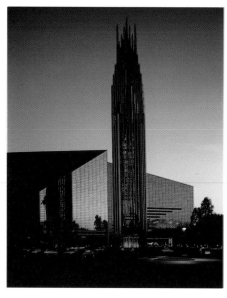

Philip Johnson. Garden Grove Community Church ("Crystal Cathedral"), California. 1977–80

Modern Art. Barragán was truly an artist of a high poetic order whose work combined the abstraction of international modern art and architecture with memories and echoes of Mexican and other traditions. By a curious coincidence Barragán, like Johnson, had absorbed much from Mies van der Rohe, but in quite another way, extending this inheritance to create precincts of haunting silence, such as his own house in Tacubaya, Mexico City (1947), or, in Atizapán de Zaragoza, the geometrical planes and water channels of Las Arboledas (1958–61) and Los Clubes (1967–68), equestrian complexes that took on the character of mythical landscapes. Where Johnson was at best an elegant stylist (at worst verging on camp), Barragán was a metaphysician who probed hidden presences with the aid of a resonant abstraction.[6]

One of the founding principles of the Pritzker Prize had been the recognition of major contributions to "the art of architecture."[7] There was something deliberate in the use of that word "art," as if to say that the aesthetic component in architecture had been mislaid or devalued by other considerations, such as social planning ideology, pragmatic functionalism, or the pursuit of profit. But the emphasis upon "art" made the prize peculiarly vulnerable to some of the passing fads of the 1980s, a period that suffered from an excess of form for form's sake. The recurrent obsessions with the past and with communication sometimes translated into facile manipulations of architectural signs and references that contained no deeper content. Alongside the postmodernist transfer of historical images there emerged neomodernisms of several kinds, which took over clichés of earlier modern architecture and reduced them to pleasing but superficial compositions of empty shapes. Devaluation may take diverse forms.

The selection of James Stirling as Pritzker laureate in 1981 occurred within the general atmosphere of a reevaluation

of the role of both historical precedent and the urban context in architecture. Stirling was the man of the moment who seemed able to straddle several positions in his work and in his architecture. In his acceptance address he stated: "I think the mainstream of architecture is usually evolutionary, and though revolutions do occur along the way (and the Modern Movement was certainly one of them, as was the time of Brunelleschi), nevertheless they are minority occasions. Today we can look back and regard the whole of architectural history as our spectrum – including most certainly the Modern Movement, High Tech and all."[8] Stirling also suggested that "representational" as well as "abstract" elements could be incorporated in the same work. The building that summed up these positions was in progress when Stirling received the prize: it was the Neue Staatsgalerie in Stuttgart (designed with Michael Wilford and completed in 1983). This combined a "collage" of neoclassical Corbusian, "post-mod" and "high-tech" devices in a populist urban monument. It was mannerist in the true sense: taking over types and tropes from the classical tradition and the earlier modern movement and inverting them in a self-conscious display of erudition; it also embodied some of the limitations of this position.[9]

Such was the mood of the times. The intellectual cousin of the Staatsgalerie was perhaps Hans Hollein's museum in Mönchengladbach, Germany, a contemporary work (completed in 1982) that was conceived as a cascading urban landscape filled with complex fragments and allusions. Hollein received the Pritzker Prize in 1985. The brochure made much of his Viennese identity, and in his acceptance address Hollein himself expressed his desire to combine "the permanent" and "the ephemeral": "Maybe this is a very European, very Viennese way of looking at things. This dualistic approach, this Manichean view, has its correspondence in the position of standing with one leg in the old world, in tradition, and with the other in the new world, in the future."[10] When one looks back with a distance of a decade and a half, the distinction between the ephemeral and the permanent makes itself felt. Can one really say of Hollein's shop designs (much published at the time) that they make any long-term contribution to twentieth-century architecture?

Curiously, two of the catalyst figures in the reconsideration of the past had to wait until the early 1990s to receive the recognition of the Pritzker Prize: Aldo

Venturi, Scott Brown, and Associates. Fire Station No. 4, Columbus, Indiana. 1965–67

Pei Cobb Freed and Partners. East Building, National Gallery of Art, Washington, D.C. 1968–78

Rossi, author of the influential *L'Architettura della città* (1966), who received the award in 1990; and Robert Venturi, author of the equally influential *Complexity and Contradiction in Architecture* (1966), who won the prize in 1991.[11] In his writings and drawings, Rossi had insisted upon the role of memory in design and upon the importance of long-standing typologies in the urban structure as a basis for transformation. Arguably his theories were more effective than his forms. Rossi's writings contributed to a reevaluation of the historic city, to a reaction against clean-sweep urban renewal, and to a rejection of simplistic functionalist doctrines, but his actual buildings have not stood the test of time so well. Some of his late works (for example, the Carlo Felice Theater in Genoa [1983–90], with its heavy-handed forms and its out-of-scale fly tower) run counter to the very civic sensitivities he himself championed.

Most architects' oeuvres are uneven, and nearly every one of the Pritzker laureates has constructed duds at some point or another. This raises the question: Just what is being honored? The aura of a reputation? The best works by an architect? A critical position as represented in writings? Venturi is a case in point. There can be no doubting the impact of his books, but do his buildings match up to the theoretical intentions? Beyond the intellectualizations, how powerfully do they speak the language of *architecture*? It is quite instructive to revisit some of Venturi's earlier realizations. Fire Station No. 4 in Columbus, Indiana (1965–67), for example, retains something of its original polemical freshness at a distance of more than thirty years. But in the 1980s Venturi seemed to sacrifice some of the qualities he himself had espoused (ambiguity, tension, contradiction, complexity) in favor of a facile collaging of historical devices and images. The results were sometimes anecdotal and without the formal strength needed to touch the mind and the senses directly. More can end up being less.[12]

Venturi was the laureate of the thirteenth Pritzker Prize, but he was also the seventh U.S. recipient. This led some to believe that the prize was tilting too far toward its home ground. Whatever the truth of this charge, it is interesting to follow the North American trajectory. After Johnson, the next in line, in 1982, was Kevin Roche. To this day Roche has not received the critical and historical reevaluation he deserves. At precisely the moment he received the prize, he seemed to falter out of obedience to the latest compositional tricks and figurations, but his best works from the 1960s and 1970s combined bold geometry with an articulate sense of industrial technique. Roche was sometimes guilty of rhetorical excess (for example, the forced grandiosity of his works in New Haven, such as the Knights of Columbus Headquarters [1965–69]), but he was also capable of responding to context and program in an undogmatic yet rigorous way. For the Oakland Museum (1961–68) he evolved a scheme of low-lying terraces and interlocking courts and gardens, in scale with the neighborhood; for the Ford Foundation in New York (1963–68), a monumental atrium with a sedate sense of luxury; and for the Cummins Engine Company Sub-Assembly Plant in Columbus, Indiana (1970–73), a haunting minimalism on the basis of standardization, transparency, and neutrality of formal expression.

Next, in 1983, it was the turn of Ieoh Ming Pei, a doyen of the U.S. corporate establishment, whose East Building of the National Gallery of Art in Washington, D.C. (1968–78), confirmed a general tendency in his work toward a diagrammatic monumentality of intersecting geometries and lavish materials. Pei's architecture scarcely proposed a challenging content, and the selection seemed conservative, especially from the vantage point of those advocating greater "legibility" in buildings. Some of Pei's structures, with their large, planar surfaces, their vast areas of glazing, and their angular trusses, were obvious

targets for those critics who felt that "late modernism" was resorting to empty gestures.[13] Conscious of the onslaughts of postmodernism, Pei used his acceptance address to defend the strand of the American modern movement to which he belonged, reaching back to his formation in the 1940s at the Harvard Graduate School of Design under Walter Gropius: "I belong to a generation of American architects who built upon the pioneering perceptions of the modern movement, with an unwavering conviction in its significant achievements in the fields of art, technology and design. I am keenly aware of the many banalities built in its name over the years. Nevertheless, I believe in the continuity of this tradition, for it is by no means a relic of the past but a living force that animates and informs the present. Only in this way can we develop and refine an architectural language responsive to today's values and allow for a variety of expressions in both style and substance."[14]

But there was not, of course, any single "modern movement," and there were in fact numerous ways of extending and criticizing the diverse traditions of the modern. In the following year, 1984, the Pritzker Prize was awarded to yet another North

Richard Meier and Partners. Museum für Kunsthandwerk, Frankfurt, Germany. 1979–85

American, Richard Meier, who had an entirely different lineage running back to the somewhat formalist readings of Le Corbusier made during his youth under the tutelage of Colin Rowe. In buildings such as his Museum für Kunsthandwerk in Frankfurt (1979–85), Meier established a signature style characterized by layers of white wall planes and transparencies, fractured structural grids, interpenetrating ramps, and spaces of varying luminosity. This particular work responded intelligently to a historical context in its space and geometry. In subsequent buildings, though, Meier risked reducing his architecture to a set of predictable stylistic recipes: a decorative formula lacking either visual or ethical tension.

The recognition of Gordon Bunshaft with the 1988 award was mentioned above, but here is perhaps the place to ask why no similar recognition was made of another U.S. architect, one whose main sin was to have fallen out of fashion: Paul Rudolph. One realizes, of course, that a prize develops its own priorities, but Rudolph was possibly the most inventive architect in spatial terms of his generation in the United States, as is suggested by his Art and Architecture Building at Yale University (1958–63). It seems odd, too, that the opportunity was missed to acknowledge another key figure in the North American architectural scene, whose late years just overlapped with the emergence of the Pritzker Prize: the Spanish-born José Luis Sert, educator and practitioner, one of the few of Le Corbusier's collaborators to define a language and philosophy of his own, as exemplified by his Spanish Pavilion at the International Exposition in Paris in 1937; the Joan Miró Studio, Mallorca (1958–59); and the Peabody Terraces, Harvard University (1962–64). In addition to being an architect, Sert was an urbanist; in fact he saw no real distinction between the two realms.[15]

Here possibly was another difficulty arising from the prize's emphasis upon the "art" of architecture. Perhaps too much stress was being placed upon the individual object and not enough upon the creation of urban space and even of landscape. The bias toward artistic values also risked masking the social complexities of architecture and its diverse roles in the creation of (and sometimes the destruction of) culture. One should not forget that during the 1980s there was a widespread mood of withdrawal from social questions in architecture, which went hand in hand with a refusal to think of buildings in relation to any more general "modern project" in society. This was especially true in the United States.

Up to the end of the 1980s the North Americans selected for the Pritzker were based mostly in the Northeast. The choice of Frank O. Gehry in 1989 helped dispel the suspicion that the Pritzker Prize was blind to developments on the West Coast, though it should not be forgotten that Gehry had been through some of the vetting procedures of the Northeastern elite – exhibitions in New York, visiting professorships at Ivy League universities, and so on. The jury citation referred to his supposed "populist Californian perspective,"[16] but Gehry was scarcely an artist to fit a "localist" agenda, even if his work did seem to respond to the collisions and contrasts of the Los Angeles environment – the strong light, the standard construction techniques (wooden stud framing with attached siding, chain link, drywall), and the "bright present of the Pacific beaches."[17] The collage techniques of his architecture had a much wider and broader pedigree in the history of modern painting and sculpture (American and other), stretching back, ultimately, to the ambiguities and spatial tensions of Cubism, while his architectural absorptions included Californian predecessors such as Rudolph Schindler and Bernard Maybeck, and a personal reading of international modern masters like Aalto, Le Corbusier, and Wright.

Moreover, Gehry's intuitions about the ambivalence and layers of contemporary reality touched chords all around the world, especially for those fed up with the linguistic excesses and facile image-making of postmodernism. The American critic Ada Louise Huxtable wrote in the booklet that accompanied Gehry's award: "At a time when 'retro' reigns, he follows the modernist route of an original vision that postmodern traditionalists have tried so hard to give a bad name. He takes chances; he works close to the edge; he pushes boundaries beyond previous limits. . . . For Frank Gehry, these explorations characteristically take place at the point where architecture and sculpture meet in anxious and uneasy confrontation. . . . He practices architecture in the most timeless and sophisticated sense, but with a very special spin. The spin is that Gehry's work goes to the heart of our time, carrying the conceptual and technological achievements of modernism (as real and instructive as its much better publicized failures) to the spectacularly enriched vision that characterizes the 1990s. He builds on the liberated 'box' that Frank Lloyd Wright broke open forever, and the liberated spaces that Le Corbusier raised to luminous heights (Ronchamp humbles us all, he says). Gehry continues and personalizes the twentieth-century tradition."[18] These were high claims indeed, but they seem justified, especially in the light of Gehry's later Guggenheim Museum in Bilbao (1992–97), truly one of the masterpieces of recent times.[19]

Works of real interest seem to occupy time in several ways: they give shape to the cultural aspirations (and conflicts) of their historical moment, but they also contain numerous echoes from the past. In honoring the Japanese architect Kenzo Tange in 1987, the prize was acknowledging a figure who had already absorbed the implications of the modern movement before the war, and whose postwar buildings grappled with the problem of synthe-

sizing modernity and Japanese tradition. The high point of this phase was the main stadium of the National Gymnasiums in Tokyo (1961–64), a feat of spatial and structural invention that fused a certain Corbusian plasticity and sense of space with the evocation of ancient temple roofs. The building was on the knife edge between national and international expression, and was a fitting monumental symbol for the Tokyo Olympic games and the place of modern Japan in the "family" of democratic nations. To move forward twenty-five years to the Tokyo City Hall Complex (1986–91) with its skin-deep international corporate clichés is to confront the evidence of a problematic decline.

The next Japanese architect to receive the Pritzker Prize, in 1993, was Fumihiko Maki, who was born a generation later than Tange, and whose formation therefore belonged to the postwar years of reconstruction. Maki's education and culture were cosmopolitan; he traveled extensively and lived and taught in the United States before returning to Japan. His synthesis included a subtle reading of the complexities of metropolitan sprawl, with a clear constructive rationalism and a certain poetry of light and materials. Maki was old enough to feel the full force of the modern masters yet young enough to absorb the critiques of ensuing generations, especially where the search for urban identity was concerned. But he also responded to the almost unconscious continuities of a Japanese modern tradition. His Fujisawa Municipal Gymnasium (1980–84) extended some of the lines of research set in place by Tange and others, while alluding in its shining metallic roofs both to the technological prowess of modern Japan and to traditional forms.[20]

The third Japanese architect to receive the Pritzker Prize, in 1995, was Tadao Ando, who, born in 1941, was some fifteen years younger than Maki. His architectural language combined a stern

Kenzo Tange. Main stadium, National Gymnasiums, Tokyo, Japan. 1961–64

Tadao Ando. Church on the Water, Tomamu, Hokkaido Prefecture, Japan. 1985–88

Alvaro Siza. Swimming Pool Complex, Leça da Palmeira, Portugal. 1961–66

minimalism in polished, naked concrete with a supreme sensitivity to light and shadow, the human figure in movement, and the articulation of space in city or in country. Ando's reaction to the chaos and cacophony of the modern information city was to produce precincts of contemplative calm – such as the masterly Koshino House in Ashiya, Hyogo (1979–81) – that allowed a reconnection with nature. Again, this was a Japanese architect with a broad, international culture (having absorbed lessons from sources as diverse as Le Corbusier, Kahn, Mies, Barragán, and Finnish modernism) who also probed philosophical concepts and aesthetic values in the traditions of his own country. Ando himself suggested that "Architecture of this sort is likely to alter with the region in which it sends down roots; . . . still it is open in the direction of universality."[21] It has to be said that Ando's architecture has been more successful at small and medium scale; his language has not adapted so well to buildings of larger size.

The Pritzker Prize has all the allure of a major international award, but has its geographical range been truly global? It is true that it has so far acknowledged two Latin American architects as well as three Japanese, but its purview does seem somewhat limited to the values of the "more advanced industrial nations." Some of the safe names of the Western world have been honored, while probing architects of the "developing world," such as Balkrishna Doshi in India, Eladio Dieste in Uruguay, or Rogelio Salmona in Colombia, have not. Indeed, in Mexico in the generation after Barragán there are at least two practitioners of international calibre: Ricardo Legorreta and Teodoro González de León. It is as well to remember that the critical apparatus of contemporary architecture, as well as the historiography of modern architecture, still have built-in territorial biases. Works like Doshi's "Sangath" in Ahmedabad (1979–81), or Salmona's official presidential guesthouse

in Cartagena de Indias, Colombia (1978–81), are in a modern tradition yet respond to their respective climates and local cultures on several levels; in terms of quality they will stand alongside anything produced elsewhere at the same time.[22]

During the 1990s the Pritzker awards have been far less centered on the United States than was the case in the 1980s. They have also responded to changes in attitude that have reduced the obsession with the past and opened the way to new sorts of abstraction, responsive to nature and to topography. This was surely part of the significance of choosing the Portuguese architect Alvaro Siza in 1992. His best buildings, including his early Swimming Pool Complex in Leça da Palmeira (1961–66) or his recent Galician Center for Contemporary Art in Santiago de Compostela, Spain (1988–93), take on the character of fields of spaces attuned to both natural and urban surroundings – social landscapes of a kind, combining fragments, routes, and levels. Moreover, Siza came from a country that was relatively marginal with respect to the major centers of fashionable opinion, and he provided an example of a committed modern architect with an allusive language capable of dealing with a multiplicity of local conditions. "Architects invent nothing," suggested Siza, "They work continuously with models which they transform in response to the problems they encounter."[23]

It is interesting that, up to now, the Pritzker Prize has stayed away from the deconstructivist neo-avant-garde, with its fundamentally cynical positions, preferring to honor architects with an open commitment to the institutional and cultural role of architecture. It was no surprise, then, when the Spanish architect José Rafael Moneo was selected in 1996, for here was a person with faith in the continuity of the city, and with a strong sense of place, who was just modern enough to appeal to modernists and just traditional enough to appeal to traditionalists. Moneo is an eclectic in the full sense – capable of fusing diverse historical types and models into new amalgams. His National Museum of Roman Art in Mérida (1980–85) distilled the memories of the place in a work of haunting, tectonic presence; it evoked simultaneously Roman engineering and the complexities of space found in Spanish Arabic monuments such as the Mezquita in Cordoba. At a time when many other architects are preoccupied with the no-man's land of the urban periphery, Moneo has really been most at home in the dense, historical urban core, as illustrated by his recently completed Museums of Modern Art and Architecture in Stockholm, whose top-lit pavilions blend with the setting.[24]

The selection of Christian de Portzamparc in 1994, Fehn in 1997, and Renzo Piano in 1998 only served to underline the pluralism of the Pritzker Prize, as each of these figures incarnated entirely different conceptions of architectural culture while continuing to draw upon and transform a diverse modern architectural heritage. Portzamparc's Cité de la Musique at Parc de la Villette in Paris (1984–95), one of former president François Mitterrand's *grands projets*, has recourse to the devices of Le Corbusier's *architecture acoustique* in marking off an urban portico to a public institution, while the rear parts of the building depart in a whimsy of curves and pirouettes. Fehn's Glacier Museum in Fjaerland, Norway (1989–91), is like a splintered piece of landform, responding to the natural forces of its Nordic setting. Piano's International Airport in Kansai (1988–94), on an island off Osaka, Japan, combines high craft and high tech in a synthesis of impressive aviomorphic profile defined by sight lines, the flow of air, the needs of circulation, and the search for an appropriate image. Here nature and the machine come together on special terms.[25]

The Pritzker Prize was founded to honor and encourage quality in "the art of architecture." These worthy aims have been furthered by recognizing individual architects rather than individual buildings, and this has sometimes introduced a note of confusion, for most of the people selected have had low points, as well as high, in their artistic careers. Moreover, the sacralization of talent runs the risk of playing directly into a star system that corresponds to the internationalization of markets and advertising in most realms of activity in the global economy. Recognition can lead to a facile success in which quantity rather than quality may reign, and in which a signature style is the defining feature. By a curious paradox, the promotion of name-designers happens to correspond with a period in which architects have less and less control over the destiny of the built environment. The art of making remarkable buildings receives attention, while the art of planning and creating larger cities and landscapes is in a profound crisis.

Renzo Piano Building Workshop. International Airport at Kansai, Osaka, Japan. 1988–94

As with any important international award, there is sometimes the risk of inflation. If the Pritzker Prize had emerged twenty years earlier, it would have had to recognize the likes of Le Corbusier, Aalto, Mies van der Rohe, or Kahn. This lineage would have made the task of later selections virtually impossible without resorting to untenable, sometimes absurd comparisons. As it is, in the first twenty years the Pritzker jurors have had to deal with a phase of extension and critique in which architecture has followed many routes, and in which there have been no obviously dominant positions or evident "masters." None of this is to minimize the individual achievements of the laureates; it is rather to place their contribution into some longer-range historical perspective, including that supplied by outstanding works earlier in this century and in the more distant past. After all, it is rare at any time that architecture is raised to the highest levels.

Meanwhile an emerging generation of architects waits in the wings, confronted by a world very different from that of 1979, when the Pritzker Prize began. It is a world in which traditional definitions of country and city are fast disappearing into the confusion of the technological landscape, and in which territorial boundaries, mental and political, are being redrawn; a world in which the tension between internationalization and local identities is taking on a new intensity; in which responsible action has to be taken in response to the need for harmony with the natural order. What all this may mean for architecture is unclear. But if this brief review of the Pritzker Architecture Prize's twenty-year history has anything to teach, it is surely that future inventions are liable to go on responding in unexpected ways to changing conditions, and that they are likely to go on relying upon a complex and evolving modern architectural tradition. The other lesson, of course, is that architectural quality takes diverse and unpredictable forms.

Notes

1 For surveys of Pritzker laureates, most useful are the annual brochures, *The Pritzker Architecture Prize*, published by the Hyatt Foundation, Los Angeles, and since 1992 by Jensen and Walker, Los Angeles.

2 See Philip Jodidio, "Vous avez dit Sverre Fehn?" *Connaissance des arts*, May 1997, no. 539, p. 14.

3 For an attempt at righting "exaggerated claims," see, for example, William J. R. Curtis, "Contemporary Transformations of Modern Architecture," *Architectural Record*, June 1989, pp. 108–17.

4 On the dynamics and pluralism of modern architectural tradition see, for example, William J. R. Curtis, *Modern Architecture since 1900*, 3d ed. (London: Phaidon, 1996).

5 Philip Johnson, "Acceptance Address," in *The Pritzker Architecture Prize, 1979: Philip Johnson* (Los Angeles: Hyatt Foundation, 1979).

6 On the beauty of Barragán's ideas, see Luis Barragán, "Formal Address, Dumbarton Oaks, Tuesday, June 3, 1980," in *The Pritzker Architecture Prize, 1980: Luis Barragán* (Los Angeles: Hyatt Foundation, 1980); on abstraction, see William J. R. Curtis, "Laberintos intemporales: La Obra de Luis Barragán," *Arquitectura y vivienda*, July 1988, pp. 18–23; repr. in *Vuelta* (Mexico City), Feb. 1989, pp. 59–62.

7 This emphasis on the "art of architecture" is recurrent in the essays of the brochures of the Pritzker Prize, from the beginning onwards. The point was reiterated, for example, in "History of the Pritzker Architecture Prize," in *The Pritzker Architecture Prize, 1995: Tadao Ando* (Los Angeles: Jensen and Walker, 1995): "The Pritzker Architecture Prize was established by The Hyatt Foundation in 1979 to honor annually a living architect whose built work demonstrates a combination of those qualities of talent, vision, and commitment, which has produced consistent and significant contributions to humanity and the built environment through the *art of architecture.*"

8   James Stirling, "Acceptance Address," in *The Pritzker Architecture Prize, 1981: James Stirling* (Los Angeles: Hyatt Foundation, 1981).

9   See William J. R. Curtis, "Virtuosity Around a Void," *Architectural Review,* Dec. 1984, pp. 41–47.

10 Hans Hollein, "Acceptance Address," in *The Pritzker Architecture Prize, 1985: Hans Hollein* (Los Angeles: Hyatt Foundation, 1985).

11 Aldo Rossi, *L'Architettura della città* (Padua: Marsilio, 1966; English ed., Cambridge, Mass.: M.I.T. Press, 1982). Robert Venturi, *Complexity and Contradiction in Architecture* (New York: The Museum of Modern Art, 1966).

12 On the question of anecdotal excess in Venturi's work, see William J. R. Curtis, "Clipper Class Classicism, Venturi's National Gallery Extension," *Architects Journal* (London), June 17, 1987, pp. 24–29.

13 See, for example, the critical writings of Charles Jencks in this period, such as "Post-Modern Classicism," *Architectural Design* vols. 5–6 (London: A. C. Papadakis, 1980).

14 Ieoh Ming Pei, "Acceptance Address," in *The Pritzker Architecture Prize, 1983: Ieoh Ming Pei* (Los Angeles: Hyatt Foundation, 1983).

15 Even today Sert awaits a proper historical and critical evaluation. He has undoubtedly suffered from having a career cut into "pieces" corresponding to different phases of his expatriate existence.

16 See "Jury Citation," in *The Pritzker Architecture Prize, 1989: Frank Owen Gehry* (Los Angeles: Hyatt Foundation, 1989).

17 This felicitous phrase is found in David Cohn, "Singing the Light Electric," *El Croquis,* vol. 45, 1990, "Frank Gehry," p. 120.

18 Ada Louise Huxtable, "On Awarding the Pritzker Prize, 1989, Frank Owen Gehry," in *The Pritzker Architecture Prize, 1989: Frank Owen Gehry.*

19 For the Guggenheim in Bilbao, see William J. R. Curtis, "The Unique and the Universal: A Historian's Perspective on Recent World Architecture," *El Croquis,* vols. 88–89, May 1998, "Worlds One," pp. 19ff.

20 See Fumihiko Maki, "New Directions in Modernism," *Space Design,* vol. 256, Jan. 1986, special issue, "Fumihiko Maki, 1979–1986," pp. 6ff.

21 Tadao Ando, "From Self-enclosed Modern Architecture Toward Universality," *The Japan Architect*, vol. 301, May 1982, pp. 8–12.

22 See, for example, full discussion of Doshi's "Sangath" in William J. R. Curtis, *Balkrishna Doshi: An Architecture for India* (Ahmedabad and New York: Mapin and Rizzoli, 1988).

23 Alvaro Siza, "Interview," *Plan Construction PAN*, May, 11, 1980; for topographical aspects of Siza's work, see William J. R. Curtis, "Alvaro Siza, An Architecture of Edges," *El Croquis*, vols. 68–69, 1994, "Alvaro Siza."

24 For the strengths and weaknesses of Moneo's position, see William J. R. Curtis, "Pieces of City, Memories of Ruins," *El Croquis,* vol. 66, 1996, "Rafael Moneo." Moneo's occasional overadherence to typological models has led to some lifeless designs, such as the airport in Seville.

25 For a discussion of changing concepts of "nature" in the recent past, see Curtis, *Modern Architecture since 1900*, 3d ed., esp. ch. 35.

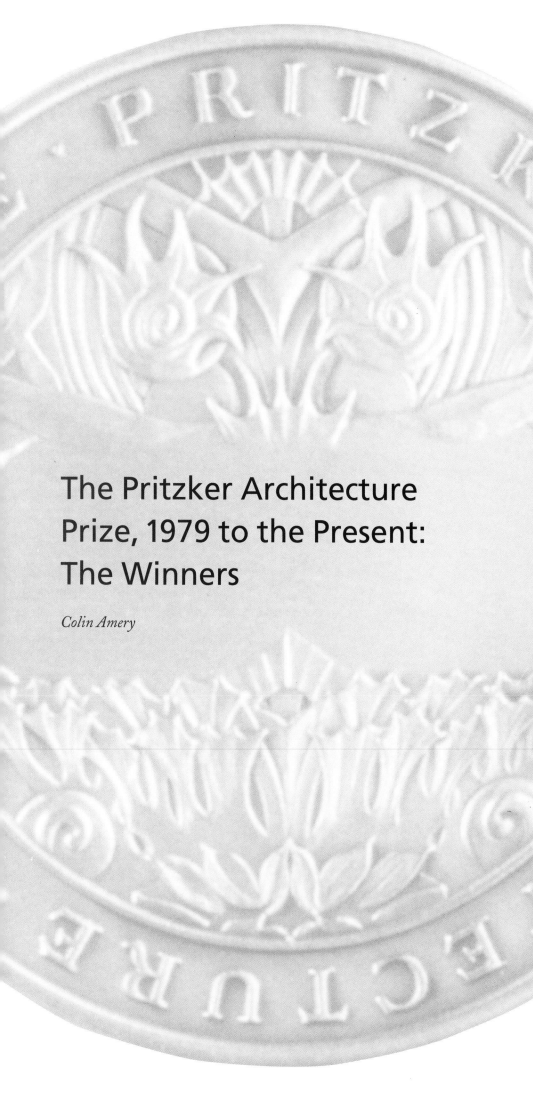

The Pritzker Architecture Prize, 1979 to the Present: The Winners

Colin Amery

Introduction

Giving prizes away is not easy. When the Pritzker Architecture Prize was announced in 1979, it was hailed as a major international exercise to raise architectural standards and as a timely marker for achievement. Architecture is a lifetime's work, and there was no significant prize that recognized the masters of the art and awarded the laurel crown. There were Nobel Prizes for literature, science, and to reward peacekeeping efforts in our troubled world, but no one had singled out that most difficult of the arts – architecture. The gift of a prize – the Pritzker is generously supported by the Hyatt Foundation – is inevitably the result of a selection process, and making winners also means having losers. To choose an architect from the hundreds that are nominated each year is the difficult part.

The prize is for the "art of architecture," and in the twenty years that the prize has been running, it is fair to ask, To what degree do the laureates represent the flowering of the art of architecture in the latter part of the twentieth century? The exhibition at the Art Institute of Chicago will give a wide public a chance to judge how representative the selection has been, how catholic, and indeed, how fair. Jay Pritzker, president of the Hyatt Foundation, has rightly said that the quality of the prize depends upon the quality of the jury. The Pritzker jury has always been of exceptional quality, and its members have devoted both time and energy to ensuring that they choose wisely. Many of the jurors are distinguished architects – but architects alone would not have been enough. It is always a difficult business for members of the same profession to reward their peers or indeed their competitors. Distinguished critics and men and women of culture and business have always balanced the Pritzker jury.

I recall the very first announcement in 1979 telling the world that the Pritzker was about to happen and talking in London to Lord Clark, who was on the original jury. Kenneth Clark in those days was always known as Lord Clark of Civilization as a tribute to his triumph as the writer and presenter of a major BBC television series on the arts of humankind entitled "Civilization." We were talking about contemporary architecture, and he said he felt that you could always tell more about a civilization from its architecture than from anything else it leaves behind. I think that he felt literature and painting depend on individuals, who may be highly unpredictable in their lives and in the way they use their talents. Architecture, however, is to a degree a communal art, depending on the relationship between the user and the maker. In his companion book to the television series, Clark wrote that "one of the reasons why medieval and Renaissance architecture is so much better than our own is that the architects were artists. The master masons of the Gothic cathedrals started as carvers working on the portals. In the Renaissance, Brunelleschi was originally a sculptor; Bramante a painter; Raphael, Peruzzi and Giulio Romano were all painters who became architects in middle life. Of the great architects of seventeenth-century Rome, Pietro da Cortona was a painter and Bernini was a sculptor; and this has given to their work a power of plastic invention, a sense of proportion and an articulation based on the study of the human figure, which knowledge of the tensile strength of steel, and of other requisites of modern building, do not always produce."[1]

Although the deliberations of the powerful Pritzker jury have always taken place in secret, it is known that there have been some intense discussions that have attempted to define what it is that makes an architect the twentieth-century equivalent of the masters of the past. How easy is it for architects to be artists when they are inevitably so heavily engaged in the worlds of commerce and competition as well as that of creativity? It is the geniuses who have risen to the surface that the jury has picked out as laureates. The men

(to date no woman has won the prize) are those whose creative talents have erupted in the world in such a way that they cannot be ignored. Their buildings have been seminal and influential. The architects have been imitated and admired in a manner that has made them both kings and kingmakers.

There is a danger in prizes. They can be awarded on the basis of fashion, and they can create style because people feel that they should copy winners. They can also create a kind of safe establishment of the approved – or a blind alley of the blessed. I do not think that the Pritzker Prize has done this. Within the Pritzker pantheon to date are twenty-one architects (in 1988, two were honored jointly), and they are remarkable for their differences. It is hard to say that they represent one architectural fashion rather than another, or that they are spin doctors of a particular style. One thing they almost all show is integrity and a belief in quality. Sometimes it is only the outrageous that gets noticed by juries. I would say that the Pritzker has, if anything, been a conservative prize. As it rewards those who have made "significant contributions to humanity and the built environment through the art of architecture," it has had to look to seasoned practitioners with a reasonable body of work. It has been a prize not for those who experiment but for those who have combined innovation and experiment with real style.

Winners

In this essay I aim to answer two questions about each of the Pritzker laureates. One: What are the precise winning qualities that each one enshrines in his work? Two: How has the laureate affected the climate of architecture as the twentieth century moves into the twenty-first?

1979 Philip Johnson

There was something almost inevitable about Philip Johnson's winning the very first Pritzker Prize. He had been for a long time the voice of architecture in America – not just through his buildings but as the key progenitor of the Department of Architecture and Design at The Museum of Modern Art in New York and as a writer and communicator par excellence for the art of modern architecture.

The precise winning qualities to be seen in his earliest architecture are a kind of derived clarity, as in his Miesian Glass House in New Canaan (1947–49), which brought the International Style to the Connecticut suburbs. His work and practice developed in all sorts of ways, including a period of rampant eclecticism for the commercial world in the 1970s and 1980s.

Johnson's skill has always been to be flexible; he has moved from international modern to postmodern in the course of his career, all while spotting talent and both encouraging younger architects and imitating them. Johnson is the perfect answer to my second question about the prize. In many ways, he has always been the barometer of architectural taste in the United States, with his genius for publicity and handling clients. He is the man who put the contemporary architecture debate onto the cover of *Time* magazine, bringing the cult of personality into the whole discussion. His win was an honor for the architect as agent provocateur.

1980 Luis Barragán

Born three years before Johnson, in 1902, Luis Barragán did not pursue publicity in his career but poetry. He was one of the most appropriate laureates because the prize did not recognize his fame as much as his immense integrity as an artist. Barragán was chosen by the jury based on his devotion to architecture as "a sublime act of poetic imagination." There are very few architects who have so clearly refined architecture down to

the essence of walls, gardens, and water bathed in clear, intense light.

Barragán, unlike Johnson, believed in God. For him, creating calm beauty where solitude enables one to achieve a sense of heavenly vision was at the core of his architectural creation. Outside Mexico City in Atizapán de Zaragoza, the water garden at Las Arboledas (1958–61), where a narrow sheet of water leads to a white wall enlivened by the shadow play of sunlit pine trees, demonstrates how architecture can create beauty by the exclusion of everything that is unnecessary. It is valuable to compare his chapel for the Capuchin convent in Mexico City (1952–55) with Johnson's Crystal Cathedral in Garden Grove, California (1977–80). Each client chose the appropriate architect – Barragán for simplicity and silence, Johnson for evangelical show business.

Barragán was not above communicating his message to the world through the medium of highly polished photography, for it conveyed, in almost abstract form, the effective poetry of his work. This was the way he raised the aesthetic temperature in Mexico and placed his vision of cosmic simplicity firmly on the world's architectural map.

1981 James Stirling

There is no doubt about the winning qualities of the architecture of James Stirling, who worked mainly in Germany and the United States as well as his native Britain. Stirling's masterpiece, the Neue Staatsgalerie in Stuttgart (1977–84), is one of those seminal buildings that occur only once a generation. It is a transitional design that takes architecture from the dogmatism of much of the early modern movement to a style that is contextual, recognizes history, and brings a sense of identifiable monumentality to public buildings. The great rotunda at the heart of the Stuttgart project brings a strong sense of formality and power into the public realm. The circular ramped space is an open route through the site, but it is

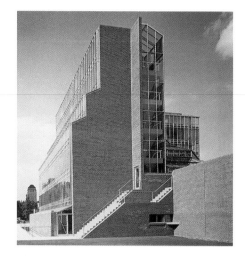

James Stirling. History Faculty Building, Cambridge University, England. 1964–67

also full of recollections of other places. It is the Pantheon in Rome as a new ruin; it is the central space of Edwin Lutyens's Viceroy's House in New Delhi, India; it is an unbuilt monument by Étienne-Louis Boullée; it is a place where history is absorbed and transformed.

The qualities of the Staatsgalerie also embrace elements of the modern movement in a way that is playful and respectful. In all his buildings Stirling was the master of the new synthesis, creating an architecture that was highly individual and never successfully imitated. The Pritzker award marked his prodigious talent in a timely way. No one was to know that his life would be tragically cut short by medical incompetence, but to give him the prize when he was only half way through his creative career was perceptive and brave, which is what prizes should be. There is no doubt that his work intensified the contemporary debate – he was both an artist and a generator of new thinking.

1982   Kevin Roche

It was fascinating to see the Pritzker jury return to honor mainstream modernism in 1982, when they selected Kevin Roche, the Irish-American architect who, with John Dinkeloo, had done so much to promote large-scale abstraction as the architectural style of corporate America. After Stirling's maverick and strange advance into the new, Roche's work had a confidence and certainty that seemed very American and very appealing. One of his best works is the Oakland Museum in California (1961–68), which is both a gallery and a garden. By putting much of the museum underground, he gave Oakland a rooftop green paradise of hanging gardens and created a sense of peace and privacy at the heart of the city. He was to continue to bring gardens into buildings: at the Ford Foundation Headquarters in New York City (1963–68), he perfected the corporate atrium greenhouse. Fiat, Union Carbide,

the Knights of Columbus, the College Life Association, the Federal Reserve Bank of New York – all were big commercial clients that needed the kind of grand and efficient anonymity he was able to provide for them.[2]

The jury's decision to choose Roche was clearly a recognition of the intrinsic splendors of his engineering and design skills – but it was also a mark of distinction for his corporate clients, who had, in selecting him, opted for a raising of standards through architecture.

1983   I. M. Pei

Born in China in 1917, Ieoh Ming Pei was to become America's most prolific contemporary architect: by 1980 his firm had some fifty major buildings to its credit. It was the East Building of the National Gallery in Washington, D.C. (1968–78), that made Pei a household name. People were fascinated to see that it was perfectly possible to add a glamorous modern extension onto a classical monumental public building. The East Building is pure Pei – but without any of the commercial restrictions that he had become used to dealing with in his years as a developer's architect with William Zeckendorf. Pei has always let his buildings talk for themselves; he has only ever been a propagandist through architecture itself. As a result he has won a quiet public acclaim that respects what he has done, which is to allow the sheer quality of geometry and space to speak their own unencumbered language.

There is, in Pei's work, an acceptance that architecture is a pragmatic art. He has been throughout his career a consummate, calm, and professional team leader, understanding all the political and social restraints that underlie any major building project. From all that complexity he has produced remarkable elegance at every turn. His skills have enabled him to move from the corporate world into the world of the great public space. Although his Louvre project (1983–93) came after

Kevin Roche, John Dinkeloo, and Associates. Knights of Columbus Headquarters, New Haven, Connecticut. 1965–69

he had won the Pritzker Prize, it stands today as a unique example of how problem solving can produce a masterpiece in what must have seemed an unbearably sensitive historical context. His rational aesthetic and his ability to find simple but effective structural solutions produce architecture that is infinitely satisfying.

1984   Richard Meier

Richard Meier answers my two questions very neatly. His winning qualities are the uncompromising integrity of his designs, which are almost ruthless in their thoroughness, and he has influenced the climate of public opinion by the clarity of his vision. I remember well our visit to his Bronx Development Center in New York (1970–77). We approached the silver building in his silver Porsche – design rigor runs through every aspect of his life – and I was carefully only allowed to look at the unoccupied parts of the hospital. This merely added to the feeling that the presence of people might spoil the purity of the design. But it is a little unfair to question purity – it is just a very difficult quality to sustain.

Meier's work grew from the seed of his early houses. A house is, in many ways for an architect, the most difficult commission. Meier's white houses in Ithaca, the Hamptons, and New Jersey are iconic in their importance. Each one is coolly perfect. They are like Bach fugues – developing harmonies through basic "notes" of space, light, and shape. They are, like their architect, intellectually rigorous. Initially, Meier's fierce addiction to the grid and to a limited palette of white porcelain enamel panels and nautical railings seems almost alien to some of the beautiful settings where he has built. But his view is that the stark presence of the houses enhances nature – and he is right. His conception of space would not have been possible without a close study of the writings and buildings of Le Corbusier, and this influence is freely acknowledged. But Meier has extended Le Corbusier's

ideas into the public realm in his museums and other arts projects. At the new Getty Center in Los Angeles (1984–97), it is possible to witness the first apotheosis of a Pritzker winner into a godlike figure. Few architects in recent decades have had such opportunities, or fulfilled them, so extraordinarily well.

1985   Hans Hollein

From the city of Sigmund Freud, Adolf Loos, and Ludwig Wittgenstein we are used to intellectual experiment. Hans Hollein is very much a son of that city, influenced by the decorative language of Otto Wagner and the Viennese Secession. Hollein is a product not just of Vienna but also of his training at the Illinois Institute of Technology in Chicago and the Berkeley campus of the University of California, where he researched the work of another Viennese, Rudolph Schindler. His Pritzker win came quite early in his career, in 1985, just three years after the completion of the Municipal Museum of Mönchengladbach, Germany (1972–82). This was not an uncontroversial museum, with its free plan and external air of a small hill town. Hollein fits into the Pritzker Valhalla because of his abilities as both an architect and a teacher. He has reexamined functionalism and, especially in his early Vienna shops and the Austrian Travel Agency (1976–78), brought back naturalistic decoration and a sense of vigor with roots in Vienna's traditions. In his work Hollein has tried to show that "everything is architecture," and his interest in the smaller elements of a room or a shop display makes his approach both thorough and somehow ephemeral. There is a richness about his designs, in his use of color and fine materials, that sets him closer to old Vienna than the New World. He has said himself that he has one leg in the Old World and one in the future, and it is as an important transitional figure in the growth of modern architecture that he was honored.

Hans Hollein. Retti Candle Shop, Vienna, Austria. 1964–65

1986   Gottfried Böhm

The award to Gottfried Böhm identified on the world stage an architect who had mainly kept to himself, working undisturbed in Germany initially – until 1955 in the practice of his father, the distinguished church architect Dominikus Böhm. After his father's death he continued to build and rebuild Roman Catholic churches in postwar Germany.

It was the extraordinary town hall for Bensberg, completed in 1967, that drew international attention to his work. A dramatic concrete tower dominated the small town, taking its place among the existing towers and medieval fortifications. Böhm was selected by the Pritzker jury for his bravery in carrying on a monumental tradition that is modern yet evocative of tradition. He celebrates concrete in majestic fashion, especially in his Pilgrimage Church in Neviges, Germany (1960–64), which some critics have placed alongside the architecture of Antonio Gaudí or even Filippo Brunelleschi for its structural invention and organic beauty.

Böhm's work is organic and sculptural but not contrived. The poetry of his buildings comes out of their structures and their relationship to their context. His more recent projects, like the Züblin office building near Stuttgart, really do conjure poetry and beauty out of steel and glass. In the case of Böhm, the prize recognized someone who had been overlooked and rewarded a talent that had been quietly laboring for his own God in the architectural vineyard.

1987   Kenzo Tange

Awards are for the work of a lifetime, and it was right to recognize the one architect in Japan who has, in the three phases of his long career, both identified and solved many of the problems of contemporary architecture and its role in modern life. Japan's postwar renewal and its unceasing awareness of the need for a national identity that kept alive its distinctive cultural values created a dilemma for architects.

Tange has solved this problem in different ways at different stages of his career. This honor marked him as a key architectural thinker of the twentieth century. His stadiums for the 1964 Olympic Games in Tokyo will always be seen as two of the best buildings of the last one hundred years. They combined Japanese traditional forms at a time and an event where it was essential to signal that country's distinctiveness – but they are also very striking modern structures. In the 1960s he became enmeshed in a group calling themselves the Metabolists, concerned with urban growth and developing the ideas of the megastructure. Tange was to move on from his early accomplishments, and his subsequent high-rise hotels and the towering Tokyo City Hall Complex (1986–91) are infinitely less distinctive. At the awards ceremony in Louis Kahn's Kimbell Art Museum, Tange mused about the future of architecture in the information age, but his prize was for past achievements because he had made some masterpieces for a transforming society.

Gottfried Böhm. WDR Radio Station Headquarters, Cologne, Germany. 1993–96

Oscar Niemeyer. Sketch of proposed buildings at Pampulha, Belo Horizonte, Minas Gerais, Brazil. 1940. The casino is at the upper left

1988 Gordon Bunshaft and Oscar Niemeyer

When these two distinguished elderly architects were honored, the jury's spokesperson, the powerful critic and author Ada Louise Huxtable called the award "a revisionist gesture" and "more of a radical than a reactionary act." In a way she was right. The Pritzker jury was demonstrating that it was trying to correct the balance. The flaws in modernism had been endlessly pointed out, but it was not right to ignore the lifetime work of two serious old hands. One of them, Gordon Bunshaft, through his firm, Skidmore, Owings, and Merrill, had perfected the corporate palaces of capitalism with lasting dignity. The other winner, Oscar Niemeyer, had to be singled out not so much for creating Brasília but for his wit and elegance with reinforced concrete and his concern with making a distinctive beauty for our century. These two prizes were justified by the need to recognize the quality of the oeuvres of two long careers and to mark them as part of history. They also elevated the fairness of the prize.

1989 Frank O. Gehry

It is art . . . no question. The Pritzker jury took a risk with Gehry because he was only halfway through his career and they wanted to encourage his obvious originality and talent. It is clear that the jury was exhilarated by Gehry's work and saw him as a kind of enfant terrible or wunderkind. Would he continue to grow and get better or would he simply become more eccentric and lose his architectural way? The truth about Gehry is that he is one of the most adventurous and talented architects around, but he is really a sculptor. What he is doing is brave and not without its dangers to the public. The jury was justified in its boldness because Gehry was to go on to design and build the Guggenheim Museum in Bilbao, Spain, which opened to great acclaim in 1997. It has fulfilled the promise the jury saw in the Vitra International Furniture Manufacturing Facility and Museum in Weil-am-Rhein, Germany, and some, but not all, of Gehry's early work.

Gehry has been both a mold breaker and a builder on the technological advances of modernism. Was there any danger that the Pritzker Prize would drag him screaming into the mainstream architectural establishment? Yes, but it was minor, for Gehry is his own man, an artist of integrity who is prepared to face failures as well as triumphs. His influence is harder to judge because he cannot be successfully imitated and he is not just the fashion punk that he sometimes pretends to be for the media. He is now bringing sculpture and architecture together, and his romantic vision is both enriching the architectural debate and giving us all an adventurous ride. What more can one ask of a Pritzker laureate?

1990 Aldo Rossi

Aldo Rossi is one of those architects who are respected for their uniqueness. His influence has been largely cerebral despite the fact that he built a great deal. His work is so very Italian and so very time-

Frank O. Gehry and Associates. Vitra International Furniture Manufacturing Facility and Museum, Weil-am-Rhein, Germany. 1986–96

less. Without Giorgio de Chirico, he would not have existed. There are not many Surrealist architects, but Rossi was one. There is even something faintly sinister about his work – it is not just timeless, it is as though time stood still. There was that uncanny moment when his wooden Teatro del Mondo floated among the spires and domes of Venice at the 1979 Biennale. There is the cemetery of San Cataldo in Modena (1971–84) – pristine and infinite, almost frightening in its cold order and comfortless corridors. And the Carlo Felice Theater in Genoa, where he added a giant tower onto the nineteenth-century neoclassical structure. And there are the toys, the coffeepots, and the tea services – all part of his strangely scaled world.

Rossi was a thinker and a writer – his editorship at *Casabella* gave him a platform for debate, and in his book *L'Architettura della città* he explored the problems of contemporary urbanism. His talent deserved the honor of the Pritzker Prize, while the long-term relevance of his hard rationalism remains to be assessed.

1991 Robert Venturi

Robert Venturi wrote his gentle manifesto, *Complexity and Contradiction in Architecture,* in 1966, and it took time for the world to appreciate his simple message: "More is more." He effectively ended the monopoly of modernist theory and made it possible for an inclusive and contextual architecture to begin to flourish. Venturi's own built work was judged severely, as it was inevitably seen as a manifestation of his theories. He has clearly felt unloved by the profession, and at the Pritzker ceremony in Mexico City he explained, in a cri de coeur, how much artists need support, encouragement, and appreciation. This is surely a strong argument for the prize itself.

There is no doubt about the importance of Venturi as an influencer of ideas, with his wife and partner, Denise Scott Brown. He has made the ordinary signifi-

cant and the mundane meaningful. He has been fortunate in his clients, especially his university clients at Princeton and his public clients like the trustees of the National Gallery in London, who gave Venturi a major opportunity to demonstrate both his urban planning and architectural theories in the design of the Sainsbury Wing (1986–91). I worked closely with Venturi on the building committee of the National Gallery, and like many artists he was not the easiest person to deal with. He developed a fruitful partnership with the gallery, and his building is a superb home for some of the earliest pictures in Europe. Although he would be the first to acknowledge his debt to Sir John Soane's Dulwich Art Gallery, he adapted and transformed the English architect's ideas into one of the finest sets of public galleries in the world. I had the fascinating opportunity of traveling with Venturi in Italy and witnessed the extraordinary way that he absorbed the qualities of Renaissance buildings and was then able to transform so many of their details in his own London project. It is an unusual architect who can build his complex theories and do so for a major public commission. At the Sainsbury Wing, the astonishing thing was that, after all the theorizing and debate, the moment when the great Venetian Renaissance painting by Giovanni Battista Cima da Conegliano, *The Incredulity of Saint Thomas,* was hung at the end of Venturi's diminishing perspective of columns, it looked absolutely perfect. It was, and is, an incredibly moving sight – art and architecture from different centuries in perfect harmony. Poetry took over from complex intellectualization and proved beyond all doubt the genius of Venturi.

1992 Alvaro Siza

Alvaro Siza's work in Portugal is intrinsic to that country. It is not insulting to say that much of his housing and smaller projects look as though they had always been there. Rather like the man himself, his

Aldo Rossi. *Seaside Constructions (Costruzioni balneari and Teatro del Mundo).* 1981. Ink and watercolor on paper mounted on cardboard, 14¾ x 11¹³/₁₆ in. The Art Institute of Chicago, Gift of Aldo Rossi and the Studio di Architettura through Mr. and Mrs. Jay Pritzker, 1991.154.2

architecture is low key and modest. Siza has always said that he does not invent anything, he *transforms*. What gives this work winning qualities is its intense respect for context. This is also its most influential characteristic and one from which many architects could learn. His Caxinus housing estate for fishermen, just north of Oporto (1970–72), consists of simple two-story houses, but they are the fruit of much social and architectural research. They allow for guest rooms to encourage occasional tourists, and in them Siza used only traditional local materials and colors.

Many of his schools and houses could be described as vernacular, but there is another side to his designs: they follow modernist stylistic ideas but become newly contextual. His Borges and Irmão Bank in Vila do Conde (1982–86) is a white and elegant interpretation of curvaceous thirties International Style. Siza would not claim to be a missionary architect trying to influence others. In his local dedication and awareness of community needs, he is a model for others to follow.

1993 Fumihiko Maki

Tokyo, Cranbrook, and Harvard are the roots of Fumihiko Maki's architecture. He literally bridges two cultures and, as his career has advanced, he has succeeded triumphantly in using the latest technologies to re-create a sense of Japan's great structural tradition. His winning qualities are best summed up in his own words, describing creation in architecture as "discovery, not invention . . . a cultural act in response to the common imagination or vision of the time." His discoveries have been structural – finding ways to create lightweight shell roofs; cultural – finding ways to unite the ideas of East and West; and poetic – determining how to capture light as a key element in the experience of his buildings.

He is not daunted by scale – his enormous Nippon Convention Center (1986–89), with its Wagnerian staircase,

and his Tokyo Metropolitan Gymnasium (1985–90), under its majestic roof, impress by their awesome size. But his own house and the little YKK Guest House in Kurobe (1980–82) show complete mastery of smaller scale. Maki offers to the current architectural climate a sense of total, sure understanding of the latest building technologies. With his strong discipline he is a laureate very much of the 1990s, with the entire world as his oyster and total confidence in his synthesis of skills from the traditions of the Orient and those of the modern Western world.

1994 Christian de Portzamparc

This young man (he was only fifty when he won the Pritzker) has brought a new sense of joy to architecture. He has done it by his passion for the great architecture of the modernists, especially Le Corbusier, whose ideas he reinterprets with almost unbelievable élan. It would be too easy to say that his approach brings French chic to modernism – he does more than that. Like many younger architects, he plunders the relatively recent past as a wardrobe of styles. Also like Corb, Portzamparc is a painter, and his visual sense brings light and color into his architectural equation

Fumihiko Maki. YKK Guest House, Kurobe, Japan. 1980–82

Christian de Portzamparc. Crédit Lyonnais Tower, Lille, France. 1994–99

from the beginning. At the Cité de la Musique in Paris (1984–95), there is an intelligent spontaneity about the grouping of the individual activities and buildings. The concert hall, with its ironic resemblance to the inside of the coffered dome of the Pantheon, is a rewarding and subtle blend of classical and modern architecture. There is also an unmistakable glamour about Portzamparc's designs. He brings this to his housing work, for example; especially the Fukuoka apartments in Japan (1989–91), which almost resemble, from the outside, a chic piece of Milanese furniture by Ettore Sottsass. Style has returned – the glossy magazine is here in three dimensions. Portzamparc wins the Pritzker Prize for pure pleasure in the art of modern architecture.

1995 Tadao Ando

Tadao Ando's architecture is not easy. It does not make any overtures to be liked and, at the tactile level, is not immediately friendly, being made largely of poured-in-place concrete. It is based on Sukiya traditional-style architecture – simple, spare, and elegant, almost empty houses that are filled with light. Until the modern movement, no such house existed in the West. His houses have to be seen in the context of the visual chaos of modern Japanese cities, where they are fortresses of sanity. Their open courtyards allow sun, wind, and rain to penetrate the interior, establishing contact with nature in the urban desert. In his first twenty years of practice Ando realized some sixty buildings, moving from houses to museums, churches, galleries, and shops. In all his work, concrete and light are the two key elements. One exception was the staggeringly elegant Japanese Pavilion (1989–92) at Expo '92 in Seville, Spain, which was made of traditional timber.

Ando is awarded prizes because he is an artist with an uncompromising vision. He also earns them because of his influence, which is anticonsumerist and a poetic stand against the emptiness of materialism. His houses are places of simplicity and contemplation. Although his work is not easy, it is crucial as a reminder that architecture is for people and can provide a sense of spiritual shelter from the world.

1996 José Rafael Moneo

It was in Mérida that the world woke up to José Rafael Moneo. Just from a photograph one could see that his National Museum of Roman Art in Mérida, Spain (1980–85), was a place of great beauty. Arch after arch of Roman brick, the new buildings rise from actual Roman ruins, both sheltering and enhancing them. But that was in 1980. Since then he has become an international teacher and competition winner with major museum buildings in the United States and Sweden, and a giant Grand Hyatt hotel in Berlin. His vaulted San Pablo Airport in Seville (1987–91) and his enhancement of the Atocha Railway Station in Madrid (1984–92) have made traveling into those cities elegant and efficient.

Moneo's talent is architectural courtesy and an awareness always of the spirit of the place where he is building. That may explain why it is hard to pin down a

José Rafael Moneo. San Pablo Airport, Seville, Spain. 1987–91

Moneo style – if there is one, it is a sense of appropriateness. Good manners may be out of style, but Moneo's architecture has them. All his work is restrained and dignified, beautifully built and careful of its context.

1997 Sverre Fehn

Norway is a country full of surprises, and the gentle modernism of Sverre Fehn is one of northern Europe's best-kept architectural secrets. He established his reputation when he won the competition for the Craft Museum in Lillehammer in 1949. Once described as the "Poet of the Straight Line," he has diligently and quietly pursued his own architectural path. He taught in London for many years at the Architectural Association and maintained the cause of modernism in his practice. He has built beautiful houses and many excellent museums. His life work has been to produce quiet, rational, and good buildings that relate to nature. His Cathedral Museum, in the county of Hedmark, both protects and reveals the ruins of the twelfth-century church. The simple glass and timber structure is so sensitive to the spirit of the place that the past is brought to life and exposed like an act of faith. Fehn's work is not well-known outside

Norway, and the Pritzker Prize has both honored him and given the world some valuable lessons in simplicity and non-competitive quality.

1998 Renzo Piano

Renzo Piano leapt to fame in 1971, when, with the British architect Richard Rogers, he won the competition for the Centre Georges Pompidou in Paris. It was completed in 1978. That strange and now rather dated building holds some clues about Piano. He loves construction, and his design logic underpins much of the external bravura of that structure. But he has soared ahead in the twenty years since the Paris competition – his latest major triumph being the great Kansai airport (1988–94), the largest in the world on an artificial island off Osaka, Japan.

However, Piano's skills are more subtle than these two giant projects suggest, and his other, quieter side is best seen in two buildings commissioned to house remarkable art collections. The Menil Collection Museum in Houston, Texas (1981–86), modestly constructed of wood and steel with a steel and concrete roof, is a sophisticated, cool design – nothing is overdone. Similarly under control is the Beyeler Foundation in Basel, Switzerland (1993–97), an unassuming quiet stone building set in a park.

The key to the winning qualities of Piano's architecture is its endless inventiveness. He comes from a family of builders, and at every stage in his work one senses the engineer in him, anxious to solve problems. He won the Fiat Lingotto competition to find new uses for the old automobile plant, and he is currently building a pilgrimage church in Italy and three concert halls in Rome. The scale of his practice is major, but at every level he is aware of function and beauty. There are several very large firms like his, but none with quite the inventive edge that ensures a new answer, the best answer, to every design problem. Not for nothing is his office called the Renzo

Sverre Fehn. Villa, Norrkøping, Sweden. 1963–64

Piano Building Workshop. He remains an unpretentious, hands-on designer as well as an inspired architect.

Conclusion

Pritzker laureates are so varied that the prize must be a genuinely effective one. There is a hint of a pattern, a determination to honor the great disciples of modernism – some just in time for the end of their careers. But the award also recognizes innovation and has rediscovered some lost talents. Its internationalism reflects the state of the art of architecture and its jury does the same. It is a generous and noble prize that could now be given more sparingly to ensure that it keeps its lustre. What it has done above everything else is to raise the profile of architecture as an art. That is a wonderful thing because the world *does* learn by example, albeit slowly. At every Pritzker award ceremony, it is clear that the profession is grateful for the recognition of the prize and, above all, for the discovery of those great friends of architecture, Jay and Cindy Pritzker.

The success of the prize in this respect was demonstrated at the recent 1998 award presentation held at the White House. When the president of the United States thanks architects for the contribution they have made to the creation of "our earthly home," it is clear that the profession has arrived. Even more splendid was the way that the gala event in Washington was in itself a review of the architecture of the last twenty years. Almost every artist and architect of significance was present to hear Vincent Scully speak of the need for architecture to make as much progress on the human and community levels as it has on the artistic level. It was very fitting that architects should be reminded of their responsibilities at an occasion that inspired them, as has the Pritzker Prize itself, to create wonders for humanity.

Notes

1   Kenneth Clark, *Civilization* (London: BBC and John Murray, 1969).

2   See Fiat Corporate Headquarters, Turin, Italy (1973; unbuilt); Union Carbide Corporation World Headquarters, Danbury, Conn. (1976–82); Knights of Columbus Headquarters, New Haven, Conn. (1965–69); College Life Insurance Company Headquarters, Indianapolis, Ind. (1967–71); Federal Reserve Bank of New York (1969; unbuilt).

The Laureates

Philip Johnson

Luis Barragán

James Stirling

Kevin Roche

I. M. Pei

Richard Meier

Hans Hollein

Gottfried Böhm

Kenzo Tange

Gordon Bunshaft

Oscar Niemeyer

Frank O. Gehry

Aldo Rossi

Robert Venturi

Alvaro Siza

Fumihiko Maki

Christian de Portzamparc

Tadao Ando

José Rafael Moneo

Sverre Fehn

Renzo Piano

Southeast view in fall

Jury Citation
The Pritzker Architecture Prize was
established in 1979 for the purpose
of encouraging greater awareness
of the way people perceive and
interact with their surroundings.

The first award is being given
to Philip Johnson, whose work
demonstrates a combination of
the qualities of talent, vision, and
commitment that has produced
consistent and significant contributions to humanity and the
environment. As a critic and historian, he championed the cause
of modern architecture and then
went on to design some of his
greatest buildings. Philip Johnson
is being honored for fifty years
of imagination and vitality embodied in myriad museums, theaters,
libraries, houses, gardens, and
corporate structures.

1979

Philip Johnson

GLASS HOUSE
New Canaan, Connecticut
1947–49

The design of the Glass House, according to Johnson, was really based on Ludwig Mies van der Rohe's scheme for a steel and glass house for Dr. Edith Farnsworth – a beautiful pavilion that was not completed until a couple of years after Johnson had moved into his New Canaan residence. Although the two structures are superficially similar, they differ in essential respects. The Farnsworth is asymmetrical, outside and in, while Johnson's is symmetrical outside and asymmetrical within. The Farnsworth House is raised off the ground on steel columns, while the Glass House sits firmly on a flat grassy plain with corners formed by massive steel columns. In the landscape, the Farnsworth House stands alone, whereas the Glass House was, from the start, a part of a formal composition. Johnson's house is framed in steel painted dark gray and features quite massive detailing. The corner columns,

for example, look twice as bulky in cross section as those at the center. It is an overstatement to say that Johnson sought quite deliberately to emphasize the classical presence of the building. All the steel framing in the house is visible; the secondary framing joists in the roof, between the "expressed" steel girders, are of wood. Moreover, the steel frame is not especially rigid. During construction, before the one-quarter-inch-thick plate glass had been put in place, the roof deck tended to sway sideways rather disconcertingly when one climbed onto it to enjoy the views of the landscape. The frame of the house did not become rigid until the glass was in place and braced the structure.

For Johnson it is essential to observe the way his buildings look, feel, and sound in their settings. The Glass House is the centerpiece of a complex that is still under expansion. When the house was first

Northeast view in spring

Living room

"completed," it consisted of not one but two structures – one virtually all glass and the other, the Guest House, virtually all brick. The space between the two, and the approaches to that space, seemed almost as important as the structures themselves.

Since that time, Johnson has designed and built several other structures on the forty-five-acre property: a gallery for his collection of paintings; another gallery for his collection of sculptures; a pavilion that was an exercise in arches, columns, and corners similar to those employed at the Sheldon Art Gallery in Lincoln, Nebraska; a tower that is a sculptural tribute to his old friend Lincoln Kirstein; a pavilion that serves as a study and retreat;

and a gatehouse, which will function as a visitor reception area when the property passes into the hands of the National Trust for Historic Preservation.

The Glass House and Guest House and the various sculptural pavilions surrounding them are a hugely successful exercise in the art of making space. After visiting the house in all sorts of light and weather conditions, the most vivid impressions one has are not of the buildings themselves as they appear in photographs, but of the way that they frame and articulate the landscape around them. The Glass House is really a series of frames that define the views of nearby trees and lawns, stone walls, lakes and pools, dis-

Bedroom

tant hills and far horizons. In the evening the moonlight on the nearby landscape spills into the house and endows it with an intimate glow. Each season engulfs the house and turns the views into magical reflections. The home is a stunning demonstration of the way a first-rate architect can harness the unpredictable resources of nature – light and shade, sun and shadow, clouds and mist, rain and snow, trees, flowers, stone, and grass.

Living room, view toward the bedroom

Main entrance and glass-enclosed courtyard between the towers

Main facade

PENNZOIL PLACE
Houston, Texas
1972–76

Johnson/Burgee Architects
with Wilson, Morris, Crain
and Anderson

Courtyard

View from the east

Main entrance

AT&T BUILDING
New York, New York
1979–84

Philip Johnson/
Alan Ritchie Architects

Southeast corner

Patio with sunken court

1980 Luis Barragán

CHAPEL AND CONVENT RESTORATION
Capuchinas Sacramentarias del Purísmo Corazón de María, Tlalpan, Mexico City
1952–55

What began as a modest commission to remodel an existing chapel became a larger project, which Barragán funded, to design a chapel, visitors' room, refectory, and furnishings. A high degree of consistency was achieved in the design, which brought serenity and harmony to the work. The design consists of a series of spaces that look and function differently. By modifying only a few elements and relying on changes in light, each room was enriched. In addition, latticework, wood floors, and plastered concrete walls of various colors help articulate the rooms. Throughout, austere materials and simple forms respect the tone set by the convent's inhabitants, members of a cloistered religious order.

An interior patio with a sunken court and surrounding walkway is the link between the old convent and the new chapel. There is a black stone fountain in the center of the court and a white cement cross on the wall adjacent to the chapel.

For the interior of the chapel Mathias Goeritz designed a stained-glass window. Its yellow hues add a golden light to the space, which is further complemented by the light wood floors and pale yellow walls and latticework.

View of the chapel from the altar. The choir is on the other side of the lattice

Entrance to the sacristy

Study for the altar and cross

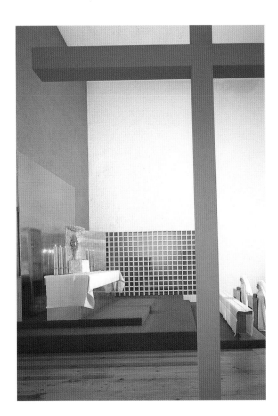

Side view of the altar toward the Transept of the Faithful

Altar, view from the alcove

Double-height foyer and staircase

Roof terrace

BARRAGÁN HOUSE
Tacubaya, Mexico City
1947

Living room, with view into the garden

SAN CRISTÓBAL STABLES
Los Clubes, Atizapán
de Zaragoza, Mexico City
1966–68

Partial view of the paddock

Waterfall and view toward the granary

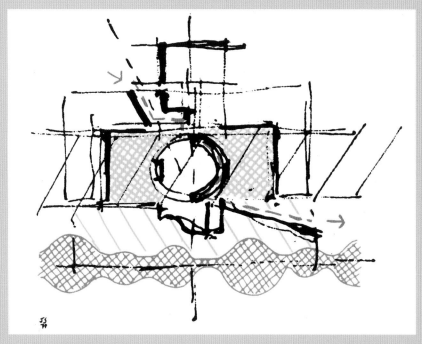

Preliminary sketch of plan

Jury Citation
We honor James Stirling – a prodigy for so many years – as a leader of the great transition from the modern movement to the architecture of the new – an architecture that once more has recognized historical roots, once more has close connections with the buildings surrounding it, once more can be called a new tradition.

Originality within this tradition is Stirling's distinction: in the old "modern times," forty-five-degree angles in plan and section; today, startling juxtapositions and transpositions of clearly classical and nineteenth-century references.

In three countries – England, Germany, and the United States – he is influencing the development of architecture through the quality of his work.

1981
James Stirling

NEUE STAATSGALERIE
Stuttgart, Germany
1977–84

James Stirling, Michael Wilford, and Associates

The new Staatsgalerie occupies a site next to the original neoclassical gallery of 1842. In an effort to reinforce the traditional relationship of buildings to street, all existing buildings on Urbanstrasse and Eugenstrasse were preserved. The entire new building is set into a hillside, with a system of terraces, roofs, and ramps facilitating circulation. The objective was to allow the public to access the new building by crossing the site diagonally, and not having to pass along the back of the building. This "urban-type" route passes at the uppermost level around the sculpture yard and down to the entrance terrace. It was hoped that this routing would encourage people to visit the galleries.

The new building is a rectangular block of travertine and sandstone comprising a peripheral sequence of spaces with an open rotunda in the center. The U-shaped plan for the galleries complements the nineteenth-century museum's symmetrical wings. The warm tones of the stone contrast strikingly with the green steel framing system of the undulating glass walls and the bright pink and purple steel handrails.

Inside, the new galleries create a sequence of well-defined and well-proportioned rooms. Endless flexible space was avoided. It is possible to make a chronological journey through the history of painting and sculpture, proceeding either from present to past by beginning in the new building, or from past to present using the original building as a starting point. A bridge connects both buildings, allowing the public to experience the old and the new without physical or psychological disruptions. The details employed, however, remind the visitor of the differences between past and present. Exposed steel beams and an industrial floor contrast with elements that evoke traditional architectural details.

Entrance hall

View from street level

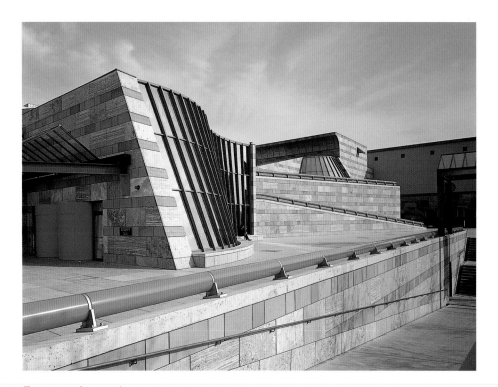

Entrance and approach terraces

Gallery

Sculpture court in the open rotunda

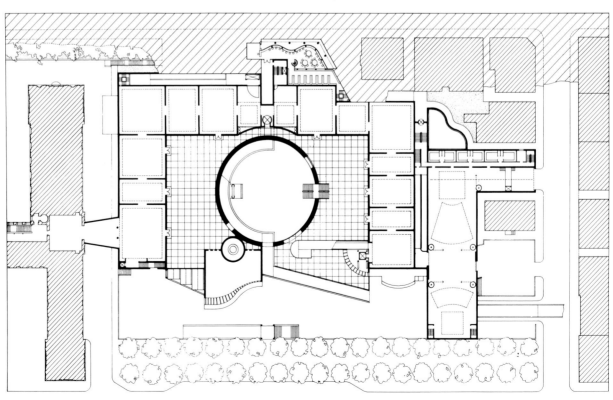

Plan, gallery level

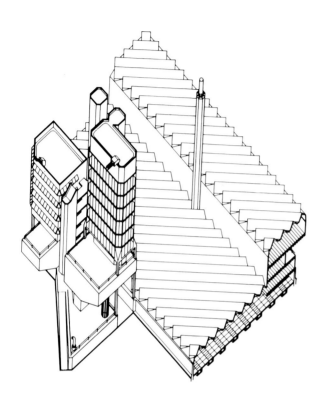

Axonometric drawing

Research laboratories (left) and office tower (right)

ENGINEERING BUILDING
Leicester University, England
1959–63

James Stirling and
James Gowan

Main entrance

TÉMASEK POLYTECHNIC
Singapore
1991–99

**James Stirling, Michael
Wilford, and Associates with
D. P. Architects, Singapore**

Junction of the library tower and horseshoe-shaped administration building

Administration building and plaza

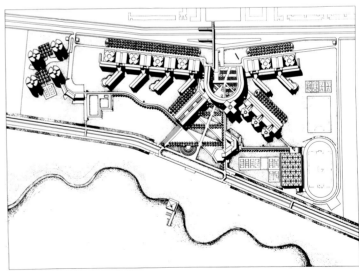

Site plan

Atrium

1982

Kevin Roche

Jury Citation
In this mercurial age, when our fashions swing overnight from the severe to the ornate, from contempt for the past to nostalgia for imagined times that never were, Kevin Roche's formidable body of work sometimes intersects with fashion, sometimes lags behind fashion, and more often makes fashion.

He is no easy man to describe: an innovator who does not worship innovation for itself, a professional unconcerned with trends, a quiet, humble man who conceives and executes great works, a generous man of strictest standards for his own work.

With this award to Kevin Roche we recognize and honor an architect who persists in being an individual, and has for all of us, through his work and his person, made a difference for the better.

FORD FOUNDATION HEADQUARTERS
New York, New York
1963–68

Kevin Roche, John Dinkeloo, and Associates

Unlike conventional New York office buildings, which isolate their occupants and store them in cubicles, depriving them of a sense of their working community and limiting their physical environment to views of other similarly stored inhabitants, the Ford Foundation headquarters provides an appropriate environment for its resident philanthropic organization. The building allows members of the foundation staff to be aware of each other and to pursue their common aims and purposes, and assists them in fostering a sense of a working family.

To achieve these goals, Roche deliberately avoided a high-rise solution. He designed a structure twelve stories high, relating to the street line on 42nd Street established by the old zoning laws, that wraps around the west and north sides of the property. The east and south sides were left relatively open to give the interior offices a view over Tudor City Park and across the East River. This plan suggested that the building could have a courtyard garden, but given New York's winter climate, it was decided to have an enclosed garden instead.

Roche employed several ascending scales in the design. The first is the human scale, which determined the office size, window size, and ceiling height. Second is the character and scale of 43rd Street, which is residential. Dark purplish granite was used to relate the buildings chromatically. On 42nd Street the scale is heroic, and the building ends the block, recognizes the park beyond, and acts as a gateway to the river.

In some respects, the third scale was influenced by that of highways and bridges – great structures of marvelous, energizing size. It seemed appropriate to adapt some of that scale as buildings grew larger and

View from the southeast

Atrium viewed from an interior office

View through the atrium and offices

larger and, as in classical architecture, to develop a progression of scales. Another idea borrowed from bridge construction is the pragmatism of bridge and highway engineers, which dictates that concrete be used as a bearing element to bring the forces right down to the ground. Steel is used as the spanning element. The Ford Foundation's stone-clad piers are of poured concrete and the spanning members are of weathering steel.

The whole design of this project emerged from a concern for the workplace, the proper placement of the building, and scale relationships to adjoining structures. There have been no changes in the use or design of this building since its completion thirty years ago.

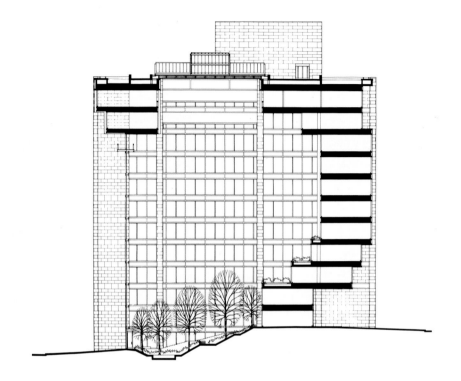

Section

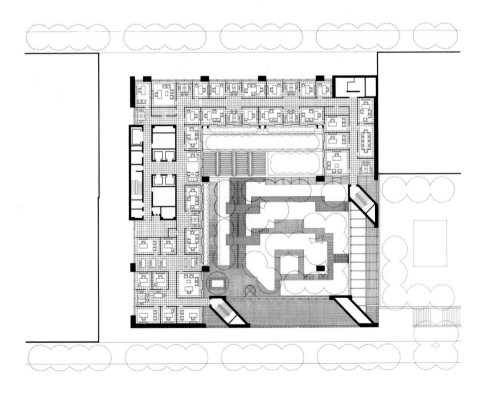

Typical floor plan

East end of the loggia

FINE ARTS CENTER
University of
Massachusetts, Amherst
1964–74

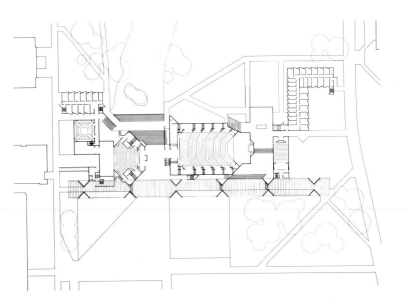

Plan, first floor

Partial view of the south facade

Aerial view

**UNION CARBIDE
CORPORATE WORLD
HEADQUARTERS**
Danbury, Connecticut
1976–82

Exterior with bridge connecting office clusters

Entrance lobby at the center of the complex

Napoleon Court with pyramid

Jury Citation
Ieoh Ming Pei has given this century some of its most beautiful interior spaces and exterior forms. Yet the significance of his work goes far beyond that. His concern has always been the surroundings in which his buildings rise.

He has refused to limit himself to a narrow range of architectural problems. His work over the past forty years includes not only palaces of industry, government, and culture, but also moderate and low-income housing. His versatility and skill in the use of materials approach the level of poetry.

His tact and patience have enabled him to draw together people of disparate interests and disciplines to create a harmonious environment.

1983

I. M. Pei

GRAND LOUVRE
Paris, France
1983–89 (Phase I),
1989–93 (Phase II)

Pei Cobb Freed and Partners

In 1981 President François Mitterrand requested that the Louvre, the central monument of French culture, be modernized, expanded, and better integrated with the city – all without compromising the integrity of the historic building. The challenge was magnified by the fact that the eight-hundred-year-old Louvre was originally constructed and utilized for most of its life as a royal palace, and was fundamentally ill-suited to serve as a museum.

Phase I of the two-phase solution involved the reorganization of the U-shaped building around a focal courtyard and the construction of a seventy-foot-high glass pyramid at its center. The pyramid serves as the new main entrance to the museum, providing direct access to previously dispersed galleries in each of its three wings. The pyramid also serves as a skylight for the 670,000-square-foot space con-structed under the courtyard to provide the museum with greatly needed technical support and public amenities: central reception, tourist and staff facilities, information desks, shops, restaurants, and a 450-seat auditorium, as well as two temporary exhibition galleries, storage rooms, restoration studios, and the newly excavated remains of King Philip Augustus's medieval palace. An open balcony with two cafés rings the Napoleon Hall at mezzanine level and provides ticketed access to the museum.

Phase II, completed for the Louvre's bicentennial, involved the conversion of the Richelieu Wing from offices of the Ministry of Finance into 387,000 square feet of exhibition space, rendering the Louvre the largest museum in the world. Unlike Phase I, which involved the construction of a new building, Phase II required the creation of new space within

Spiral stair in the main reception area, Napoleon Hall

Photomontage of the proposed Grand Louvre project in its urban context

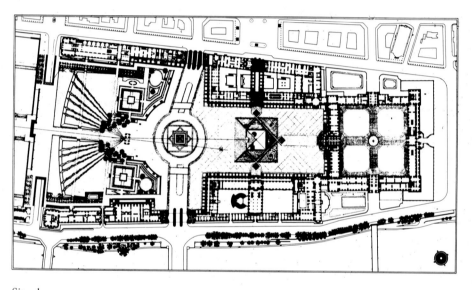

Site plan

a historic shell. Work included the cleaning and restoration of the palace facades and sculpture, the conversion of three interior courtyards (previously used for parking) into skylit sculpture courts, and the replacement of six floors of offices with three generously scaled levels for exhibiting art: French sculpture on the ground floor for maximum support, decorative arts in the middle, and painting at the top level, in skylit galleries. An innovative skylight system, which took three years to design, filters out damaging ultraviolet rays while directing light to the paintings on the walls instead of onto the floors. A grand escalator court facilitates access to the different levels, merging the old with the new and equipping the Louvre for its role as a modern museum.

Other aspects of Phase II included construction of the Inverted Pyramid (in the center of the redesigned Carrousel roadway), which admits light into the central court of the Carrousel of the Louvre, a new underground cultural and commercial complex that is supplementary to but independent of the museum. The Carrousel Terraces and Gardens have also been redesigned to form an extension of the completed Napoleon Court and historic Tuileries Gardens. Corollary goals focused on urban access and reanimation of the neighborhood surrounding the Louvre. Once a barrier to circulation, this half-mile-long building has become a vital connective tissue that offers welcoming outdoor gathering places and new pedestrian links to the surrounding city.

Skylights illuminate the third-floor painting galleries

Night view

View from inside the pyramid toward the historic palace

Exterior with main entrance arch

**MORTON H. MEYERSON
SYMPHONY CENTER
Dallas, Texas
1982–89**

Main lobby, view of the monumental stair

Concert hall

MIHO MUSEUM
Shiga Prefecture, Japan
1991–96

I. M. Pei, Architect

Main hall, view west across the valley

Perspective showing the exposed west facade, with access bridge and tunnel entrance
in the distance

Overall view showing the many skylights

Atrium lobby of the museum

1984

Richard Meier

THE GETTY CENTER
Los Angeles, California
1984–97

Richard Meier and Partners

The Getty Center occupies a unique, hilly site jutting south from the Santa Monica Mountains into the residential neighborhood of Brentwood. The program brings together for the first time the seven components of the Getty Trust into a coherent unity, and at the same time maintains their individual identities. The buildings are organized along two natural ridges of the 110-acre parcel. An intersection of the twin axes at an angle of 22.5 degrees corresponds to the inflection of the San Diego Freeway as it bends northward out of the Los Angeles street grid. An underground parking garage and a tram station establish the public entrance to the site.

The museum lobby provides views through the courtyard to gallery buildings arrayed in a continuous sequence. Smaller pavilions connected by gardens break

down the scale of the museum, allowing for pauses and encouraging interplay between the interior and exterior. A 450-seat auditorium, west of the trust offices and those of the Art History Information Program, terminates the east elevation. In designing the Getty Conservation Institute, the Getty Center for Education, and the Getty Grant Program offices, Meier took advantage of the climate through the use of loggias, pergolas, and full-height glazing along the external perimeter. Located on the more secluded western ridge, the Getty Research Institute for the History of Art and the Humanities completes the complex. It comprises a million-volume library, reading rooms, study carrels, a small exhibition space, and offices for staff and scholars. This vast reference facility has been given a more or less radial organization focused

View toward the atrium lobby from the courtyard

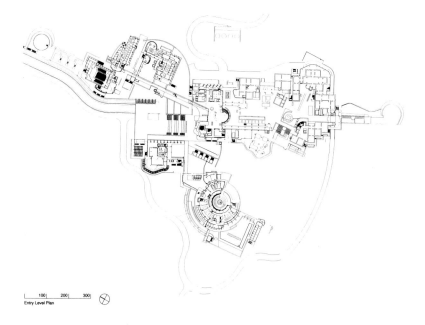

100 | 200 | 300 |
Entry Level Plan

Plan, entry level

around a central circular core. The information, however, is not centralized, but organized into a series of small sub-libraries. The plan encourages scholars to explore incidental areas in the open stacks, and its curvature expresses the Getty Center's introspective and analytical nature.

Throughout the complex, landscaping integrates the buildings into the topography with garden sequences extending beyond the enclosed volumes.

View from the east

The Getty Center. View from the northwest of the restaurant and the Center for the History of Art. March 1991 RM

Sketch, view from the northwest of the restaurant and Research Institute

Main approach to the center, with the Conservation Institute and Getty Trust offices
in the background

Painting gallery

East Pavilion of the museum

SMITH HOUSE
Darien, Connecticut
1965–67

View from the south

Living room

View from the shore

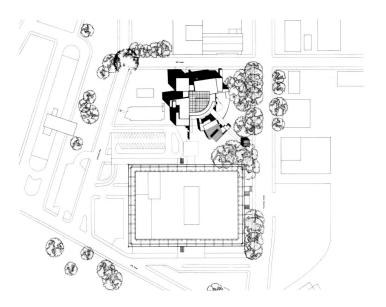

Central atrium

Site plan

HIGH MUSEUM OF ART
Atlanta, Georgia
1980–83

Main entrance

Preliminary sketch

1985

Hans Hollein

HAAS-HAUS
Vienna, Austria
1985–90

The most prominent site in Vienna, opposite St. Stephan's Cathedral, marks the south corner of the ancient Roman *castrum* of Vindobona. Thus it not only defines the transition between the urban spaces on Graben and around St. Stephan's Cathedral, but it is also of historical and symbolic significance.

The project development for Haas-Haus began with the urbanistic molding of these spaces, which previously wove around the corner in a rather unarticulated way. Various elements of the building contributed to this end, such as the regular rhythm of the large shop windows at street level, the cubic projection cantilevered out at the top to mark the main entrance, and the paving and lighting in the plaza in front of the building.

The relatively small site faces public areas on three sides. Haas-Haus is situated in the most sensitive area of the inner city of Vienna, where strict legal regulations originally forbade any modern architectural language. The design sparked lengthy debate, but in the end it led to a relaxation of the local building code and, thus, to greater tolerance of modern buildings.

The articulation of the building, both internal and external, was a volumetric issue much more than a matter of elevations. The curved stone skin partially peels off from a structural glass facade; both of these elements float above a double-story colonnade, whose scale is derived from that of the surrounding buildings. A rather calm, slightly warped stone facade faces Goldschmidgasse. Between these two facades cylindrical forms intersect with cubes and push forward above the entrance into the space between Stock-im-Eisen and St. Stephan's Plaza.

Main entrance, facing St. Stephan's Cathedral

Aerial view

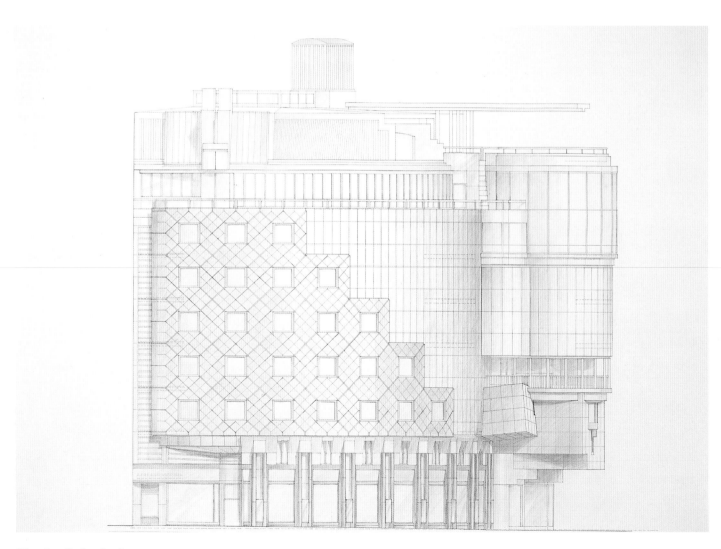

Elevation, Graben facade

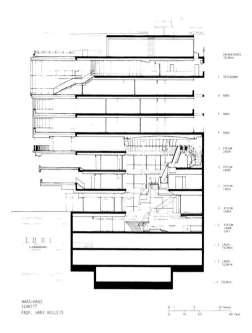

HAAS-HAUS
SCHNITT
PROF. HANS HOLLEIN

Section

Because of its location and importance, the building had to become a
public place. This corresponded to the
client's requirements for a shopping
atrium of five levels. All floors are accessible by elevators and stairs arranged in a
central core of stone, steel, and glass that
is covered by a glass dome. The three
floors above the shopping levels house
office space, and the top floor is occupied
by a restaurant that offers a panoramic
view of the cathedral.

Atrium shopping area

MUNICIPAL MUSEUM
Mönchengladbach, Germany
1972–82

View of the museum from the garden

Isometric drawing of the site

Gallery

**EUROPEAN CENTER
OF VOLCANISM**
Auvergne, France
Projected for completion
in 2001

Model

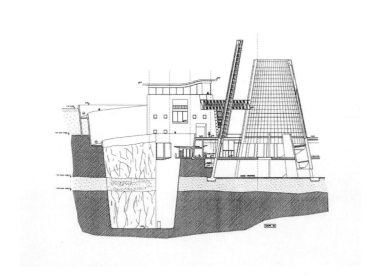

Section

Perspective sketch

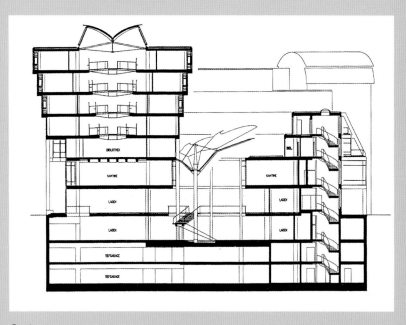

Section

Jury Citation
Son, grandson, husband, and father of architects, Gottfried Böhm has reason to recognize the nourishment that traditional ways and means provide in architecture, as in all the arts. In the course of a career of more than forty years, he has taken care to see that the elements in his work that suggest the past also bear witness to his ready acceptance – whether in the design of churches, town halls, public housing, or office buildings – of the latest and best of contemporary technology. His highly evocative handiwork combines much that we have inherited from our ancestors with much that we have but newly acquired – an uncanny and exhilarating marriage, to which the Pritzker Architecture Prize is happy to pay homage.

1986

Gottfried Böhm

**WDR RADIO STATION
HEADQUARTERS
Cologne, Germany
1993–96**

Completed in 1996, the new building of the former West German public broadcasting company WDR is situated in the center of the old part of Cologne. The site is bordered by shops and offices along Breite Strasse, traditional small lots on Elstergasse and Auf der Ruhr, and the main thoroughfare of central Cologne, Tunisstrasse, with its heavy traffic. The new WDR headquarters links former WDR buildings close by – the old headquarters at Wallrafplatz by Peter Friedrich Schneider, built in 1949–52, and its extension on Appellplatz, completed in 1970.

A main concern was to integrate the new construction into the surrounding environment by linking it to the neighboring shopping district. The retail area on the ground level invites passersby inside and forms an easy connection between the building and the street. Three passageways lead from the outside colonnades

into the central atrium, which rises from the basement, features a fountain, and is covered by a skylight. With its extensive use of glass on the interior and exterior to create transparency and openness, the building expresses its function as a public institution. Its stepped massing responds to the surrounding building heights and scale of the streets: the seven-story office wing faces Tunisstrasse, and the four-story block faces the lower-scale back streets.

In the main office section housed in the seven-story wing, work spaces are arranged on both sides of a large central skylit hall. All offices face the street and thereby allow natural light to enter and provide views of the urban activity outside. Spaces are designed for both private individual work and group collaboration, as required in a radio station. A unique system of suspended walkways and bridges

View of the office wing and its skylight

Building and arcade at night

Tunisstrasse facade

through the hall allows one to access the offices on each floor without disturbing these work areas. Glass block used in the circulation paths lets daylight filter through from the skylight to the lower floors. Glass walls between the offices and hall add to the crisp, transparent character of the building.

From the outside the central arcade is clearly visible through the entirely glazed facade. The rising wings of the skylight mediate between the different heights of the building and create a sculptural roofline. This variety of forms and spaces corresponds to the transparent and open facade, with its recesses and projections. The building's structure is suggested by a grid of concrete pillars. At the corner of Tunisstrasse and Breite Strasse the floors are skewed to form an irregular facade. They seem to launch the radio waves throughout the country, as further symbolized in the radiating pattern of the neon lights on the facade.

Ground-floor library

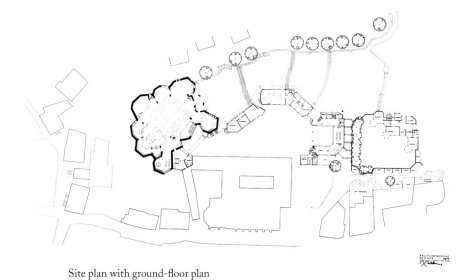

Site plan with ground-floor plan

**CHURCH OF THE
PILGRIMAGE**
Neviges, Germany
1960–64

A walkway leads to pilgrims' housing and the church

Interior view of the church showing the extensive use of concrete

Overall view

DEUTSCHE BANK
Luxembourg, Luxembourg
1987–91

Lobby

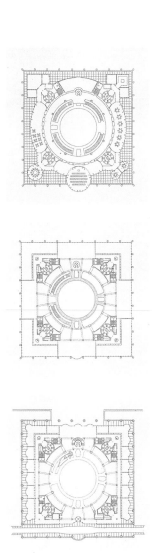

Plans: top, intermediate, and first floors

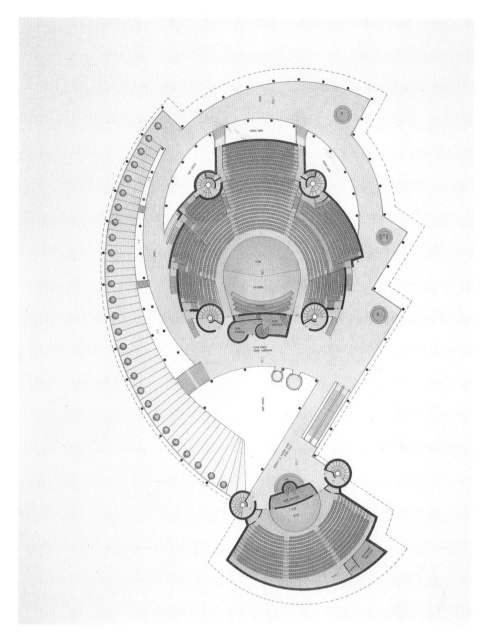

Plan

**PHILHARMONIC
CONCERT HALL**
Competition project
Luxembourg, Luxembourg
1997

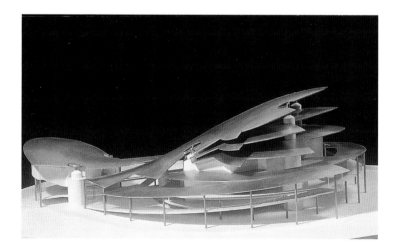

Model

Perspective, main hall

View from the west

Jury Citation
Given talent, energy, and a sufficiently long career, one may pass from being a breaker of new ground to becoming a classic. This has been the happy fate of Kenzo Tange, who in his eighth decade is celebrated as an architect of international reputation. Along with his practice, he has been a leading theoretician of architecture and an inspiring teacher; among the well-known architects who have studied under him are Fumihiko Maki and Arata Isozaki. His stadia for the Olympic Games held in Tokyo in 1964 are often described as among the most beautiful structures built in the twentieth century. In preparing a design, Tange arrives at shapes that lift our hearts because they seem to emerge from some ancient and dimly remembered past and yet are breathtakingly of today.

1987 Kenzo Tange

CITY HALL COMPLEX
Tokyo, Japan
1986–91

Kenzo Tange Associates

The new City Hall Complex symbolizes the autonomy and culture of Tokyo. The complex is divided into two administrative towers, Tower I at forty-eight stories and Tower II at thirty-three, and a seven-story Assembly Building.

The program for City Hall Tower I required a large building, but the local codes allowed a height of only 812 feet. Taking this into account Tange decided to branch the structure into two towers at the thirty-third floor to decrease its impact.

The profile of City Hall Tower II was initially purely horizontal, but after further studies Tange revised it to step downward toward City Hall Tower I, which enhanced the connection between the two buildings.

Across from City Hall Tower I are the Assembly Building and Citizens' Plaza. The plaza and its colonnade are an integral part of the complex. The surrounding high-rises create a sense of urbanism in the plaza, which is unique not only for Tokyo but for most major cities in Japan.

Tange made the office space as flexible as possible since the various government agencies housed in the complex often require reorganization. To this end he designed structural cores of 21 x 21 square feet to house staircases, emergency elevators, and mechanical equipment and to serve as a superstructure for creating flexible office space, which spans nearly sixty-five feet and integrates diverse functions into one cohesive working environment.

Tower I (left) and Tower II (right)

Tower I, lobby

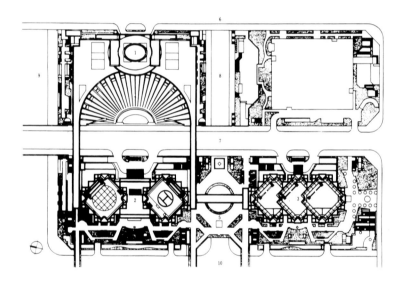

Site plan. Assembly Building is at upper left, Tower I
at lower left, Tower II at lower right

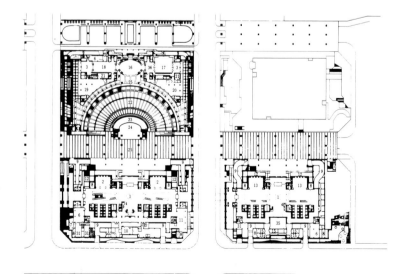

Plan, first floor

Citizens' Plaza and Assembly Building

Assembly hall

View from the southeast

PEACE CENTER
Hiroshima, Japan
1946–50

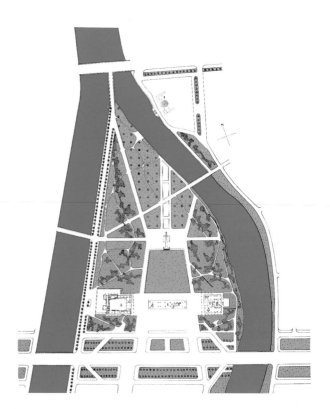

Master plan

View from the memorial dome to the museum

NATIONAL GYMNASIUMS
Tokyo, Japan
1961–64

Main stadium

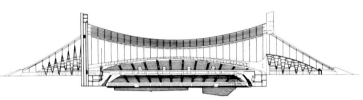

Section, main stadium

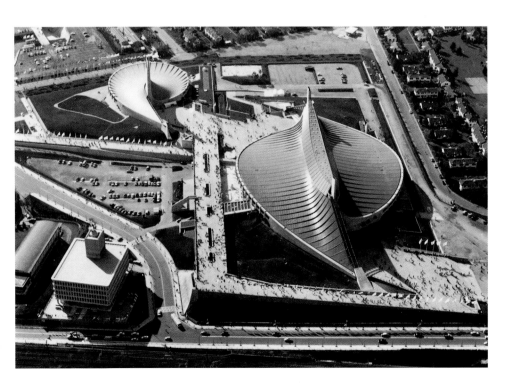

Aerial view of the two stadiums

View from southeast

Jury Citation
Gordon Bunshaft is an architect of modest claims and significant deeds. When he states that he prefers that his buildings speak for him, he has chosen eloquent spokesmen. From the landmark Lever House in New York City to his crowning achievement, the National Commercial Bank in Saudi Arabia, his forty years of designing masterpieces of modern architecture demonstrate an understanding of contemporary technology and materials that is unsurpassed.

His astute perception that architecture is a joint venture between client and designer has generated mutual respect and creative collaborations, producing great buildings with an appropriate fusion of humanity and functionality for the people who inhabit and use his structures.

Perhaps no other architect has set such a timeless standard in the urban/corporate world, one by which future generations will judge this period, no doubt with acclaim, thanks to his abilities. He has already been acknowledged by peers and critics of his own era, and the bestowing of the Pritzker Architecture Prize reaffirms his place in history for a lifetime of creativity in beautifying and uplifting the environment.

1988

Gordon Bunshaft

LEVER HOUSE
New York, New York
1947–52

Gordon Bunshaft with
Skidmore, Owings, and Merrill

The original program for Lever House called for a building to house the company's headquarters and to accommodate approximately twelve hundred employees. The structure was to contain executive and administrative offices, an auditorium, dining facilities, a reception area, support facilities, and an underground garage. Instead of including traditional lobby and commercial space, Bunshaft designed an open colonnaded space, accessed directly from the sidewalk, with a planted courtyard open to the sky. Only about 30 percent of the ground floor is interior space. The second floor seems to float above the courtyard. Above the north portion of the second floor rises a twenty-four-story tower; it is only fifty-three feet wide and is set perpendicularly to Park Avenue. The tower, its skin a grid of stainless-steel mullions that hold in place fixed panes of green-tinted glass, gives the building a crystalline quality. At night when the interior lights are turned on, the rhythmic vertical elements of the steel frame are made obvious, and each floor becomes a horizontal band of light.

The sources for Bunshaft's design are many; Le Corbusier and Ludwig Mies van der Rohe are but two. More important is the fact that in 1952 there was nothing quite like the new Lever House. It not only contrasted sharply with its stone and brick neighbors, but it was one of the first sealed glass towers built. The innovative curtain wall covering almost all of the visible facades, the integrally designed window-washing system, and the provision of public space and an open courtyard at the base enormously influenced skyscrapers to follow. Lever House was the prototype for a new era.

View from the Seagram Building plaza

Lewis Mumford stated in 1952, "Lever House is a building of outstanding qualities, mechanical, esthetic, human, and it breaks with traditional office buildings in two remarkable respects. It has been designed not for maximum rentability but for maximum efficiency in the dispatch of business, and it has used to the full all the means now available for making a building comfortable, gracious, and handsome."[1]

1   Lewis Mumford, "House of Glass," *From the Ground Up* (New York: Harcourt, Brace, 1956), p. 156.

View north along Park Avenue, showing details of the building's surface

Night view

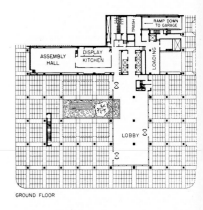

Plans: first, second, and third floors

Employee roof garden

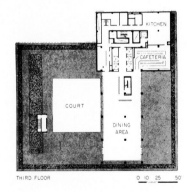

Lobby

CHASE MANHATTAN
BANK HEADQUARTERS
New York, New York
1955–61

West facade

Plaza and rock garden

Typical open-plan office floor

View from the plaza

Ground-floor reception area, showing the translucent marble walls

BEINECKE RARE BOOK AND MANUSCRIPT LIBRARY
Yale University,
New Haven, Connecticut
1960–63

Mezzanine exhibition and lounge area

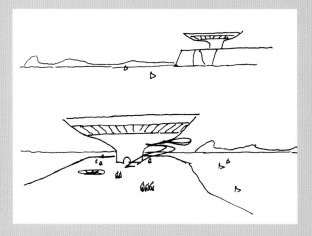

Preliminary sketches

Jury Citation

There is a moment in a nation's history when one individual captures the essence of that culture and gives it form. It is sometimes in music, painting, sculpture, or literature. In Brazil, Oscar Niemeyer has captured that essence with his architecture. His building designs are the distillation of the colors, light, and sensual imagery of his native land.

Although associated primarily with his major masterpiece, Brasília, the capital city of Brazil, he achieved early recognition from one of his mentors, Le Corbusier, and went on to collaborate with him on one of the most important symbolic structures in the world, the United Nations headquarters.

Recognized as one of the first to pioneer new concepts in architecture in this hemisphere, Niemeyer creates designs that combine artistic gesture with underlying logic and substance. His pursuit of great architecture linked to roots of his native land has resulted in new plastic forms and a lyricism in buildings, not only in Brazil but around the world. For his lifetime achievements, the Pritzker Architecture Prize is bestowed.

1988

Oscar Niemeyer

MUSEUM OF CONTEMPORARY ART
Niterói, State of
Rio de Janeiro, Brazil
1991–96

The museum, a 38,000-square-foot-building housing Brazilian art from the 1960s to 1990s in the João Leão Sattamini collection, is dramatic in form and location. Conceived of as part of a building campaign sponsored by the municipality and the ministry of culture, the design was intended to help define a new image for Niterói, which was then considered just a bedroom town of Rio de Janeiro. The museum's spectacular site, high on a cliff at the edge of Guanabara Bay, commands a spectacular view of Rio across the water and the Sugar Loaf and Corcovado mountains.

The structure has been likened in form to a chalice and even a flying saucer. In the partially underground level are located the restaurant, bar, auditorium, and services for the building. The stem rises up and flows outward into a circular volume that hovers above the ground. Offices and work spaces occupy the lower floor, and the main exhibition galleries, with a mezzanine overlooking the sea, are housed above. A curved concrete ramp winds up to the museum, creating a promenade of changing vistas.

Niemeyer has said: "Sometimes a project is difficult to define. At other times it emerges suddenly, as if previously we had carefully held it back. And this happened with the museum project. The terrain was narrow, surrounded by the sea, and the solution occurred naturally, having as a starting point the inevitable central support. From it, the architecture arose spontaneously, like a flower. The view toward the sea was extremely beautiful and had to be taken advantage of. I hung the building up, and below it the panorama stretched out even more beautifully.

The museum overlooks Guanabara Bay

Panoramic view with Rio de Janeiro in the distance

"Next I defined the museum's profile: a line that springs from the ground and without interruption grows and unfolds, sensually, up to the roof. The building's form, which I always imagined as circular, was established, and I dwelt passionately on its interior. Around the museum I created a veranda with views of the sea; this idea is echoed on the second floor, where a mezzanine overlooks the great exhibition gallery. I took pains with the interiors, wanting them to be attractive and varied, to invite visitors to get to know them better. On the terrain, my idea was to emphasize the entrance to the museum, so I designed an external ramp, a means of walking around the architecture. I felt that the museum would be beautiful and so different from the others that rich and poor alike would take pleasure in visiting it."[1]

Plaza and entry ramp

1   Oscar Niemeyer, *Oscar Niemeyer: Museu de Arte Contemporânea de Niterói* (Rio de Janeiro: Revan, 1997), p. 12.

Ramp leading to exhibition level of the museum

Gallery

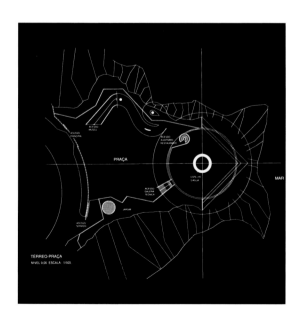

Site plan

View of the house and pool

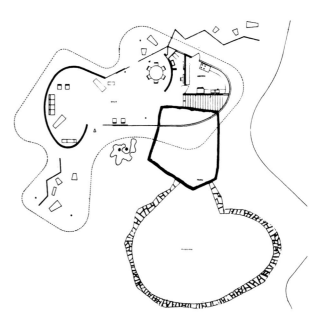

Plan, upper floor

OSCAR NIEMEYER HOUSE
Rio de Janeiro, Brazil
1953

View from the patio into the living room

View from the plaza

Cathedral with reflecting pool

**METROPOLITAN
CATHEDRAL
Brasília, Brazil
1959–70**

Preliminary sketches

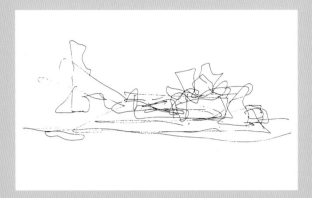

Preliminary sketch

1989

Frank O. Gehry

GUGGENHEIM MUSEUM
Bilbao, Spain
1992–97

Frank O. Gehry and Associates

The Guggenheim Museum Bilbao represents the first step in the redevelopment of the former trade and warehouse district along the south bank of the Nervión River. Directly accessible from the business and historic districts of the city, the museum marks the center of a cultural triangle formed by the Museo de Bellas Artes, the university, and the old town hall. A public plaza located at the entrance of the museum encourages pedestrian traffic between the museum and the Museo de Bellas Artes, and between the Old City and the river front.

The main entrance to the Guggenheim Museum Bilbao gives onto a large central atrium, where a system of curvilinear bridges, glass elevators, and stair towers connects the exhibition galleries concentrically on three levels. A sculptural roof form rises from the central atrium, flooding it with light through glazed openings.

The museum includes three distinct types of exhibition spaces. The permanent collection is housed in two sets of three consecutively arranged square galleries stacked at both the second and third levels of the museum. The temporary exhibitions are installed in a dramatic elongated rectangular gallery that extends to the east, passing beneath the Puente de la Salve bridge and terminating in a tower on its far side. The collection of works by living artists is housed in a series of curvilinear galleries placed throughout the museum, allowing the pieces to be viewed in relation to the permanent holdings and temporary shows.

The major exterior materials are Spanish limestone and titanium panels, the former used to sheathe the building's rectangular volumes and the latter employed to clad the more sculptural shapes. Large glazed curtain-walls provide views of the river and the surrounding city.

View down Iparraguirre Street toward the museum

View from across the Nervión River

Museum and surrounding industrial area

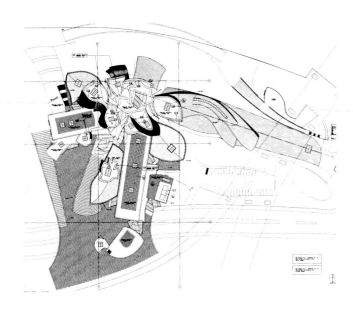

Plan, roof

Atrium

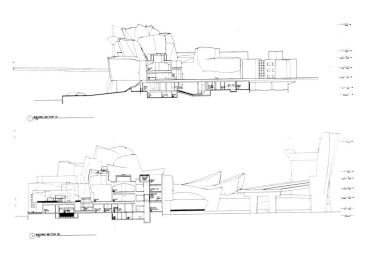

Sections

Gallery

NATIONALE-NEDERLANDEN
BUILDING
Prague, Czech Republic
1991–95

View from across the Vltava River

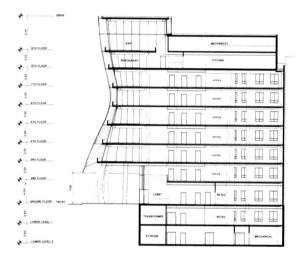

Section

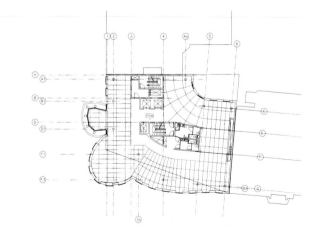

Typical floor plan

View from the east

Model, Behrenstrasse facade

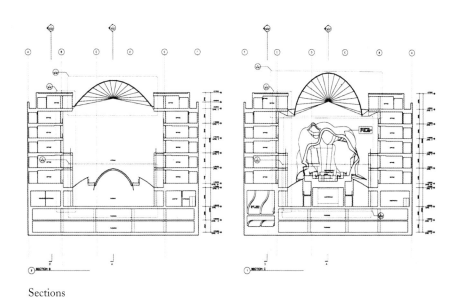

Model, atrium

DG BANK
HEADQUARTERS PROJECT
Berlin, Germany
1995–98

Sections

Interior of the cube

Jury Citation
Known for many years as a theorist, philosopher, artist, and teacher, Aldo Rossi has spent time developing his architectural voice and pen. Words as well as drawings and buildings have distinguished him as one of the great architects. As a master draftsman, steeped in the tradition of Italian art and architecture, Rossi has made sketches and renderings of buildings that have often achieved international recognition long before being built.

His book, *L'Architettura della città (The Architecture of the City)*, published in 1966, is a significant study in urban design. Out of this theoretical base came designs that seem always to be a part of the city fabric, rather than an intrusion. Each of Rossi's projects, whether an office complex, hotel, cemetery, a floating theater, an exquisite coffee pot, or even toys, captures the essence of purpose.

Rossi has been able to follow the lessons of classical architecture without copying them; his buildings carry echoes from the past in their use of forms that have a universal, haunting quality. His work is at once bold and ordinary, original without being novel, refreshingly simple in appearance but extremely complex in content and meaning. In a period of diverse styles and influences, Rossi has eschewed the fashionable and popular to create an architecture singularly his own. His influence is extensive and expands with every new commission.

1990 Aldo Rossi

CEMETERY OF SAN CATALDO
Modena, Italy
1971–84

Aldo Rossi with Gianni Braghieri

The winning entry in a national competition, the scheme Rossi created with Gianni Braghieri was to enlarge the existing cemetery in Modena. The design has been called a metaphor for the urban theories Rossi presented in his 1966 book, *The Architecture of the City*. The project for the cemetery is not so much a re-creation of the past but rather the translation of it into a modern setting. There are references to Étienne-Louis Boullée, Giovanni Battista Piranesi, and Giorgio de Chirico in the design. It also engages in a dialogue with the original Modena burial grounds, a Jewish cemetery, and a nineteenth-century neoclassical cemetery. Perhaps most important, the design represents an attempt to define a series of buildings and spaces that create a powerful overall experience for the living who visit this city of the dead.

Still incomplete, the cemetery is being built in stages, as needed by the town.

The main elements of the cemetery are identifiable, well-defined forms, stripped of ornament. They rely on collective memory and careful arrangement to communicate their message. A colonnade separates the new San Cataldo from the existing cemeteries. It also serves as a walkway and a place for flower vendors to set up their stands.

Two concentric C-shaped buildings that serve as ossuaries and columbaria frame several structures at the center of this site. Here a series of parallel rows of ossuaries is bisected by a main axis. These rows decrease in length from one end of the series to the other; when read in plan they form a triangle. The ossuaries are triangular in elevation as well: they

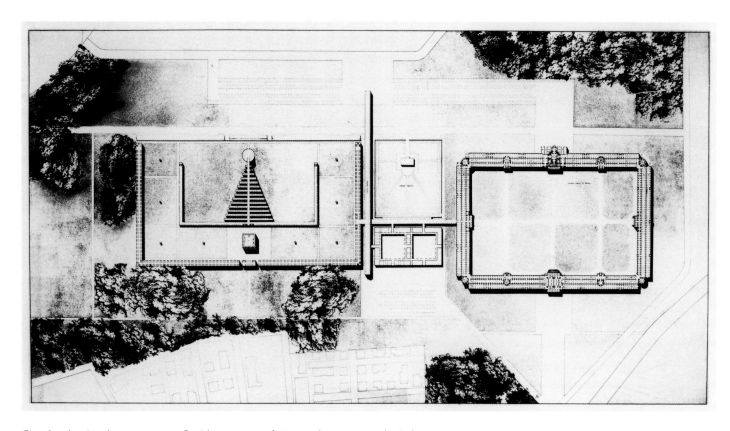

Site plan showing the new cemetery, Jewish cemetery, and nineteenth-century neoclassical cemetery

increase in height as the rows become shorter. The main axis culminates in a cube at one end and a cone at the other. The cube is a giant ossuary. The regularly placed square windows devoid of glass or shutters impart a haunting appearance to this house of the dead. The large conical structure, a reference to a factory chimney or perhaps that of a World War II death camp, is situated over a mass grave for the destitute.

Perspective drawing of the entrance and cube-shaped ossuary

Interior of one of the ossuaries

Colonnade

View from the Jewish cemetery toward the colonnade

View from the canal

Perspective and elevation

HOTEL IL PALAZZO
Fukuoka, Japan
1987–94

Aldo Rossi

Main facade

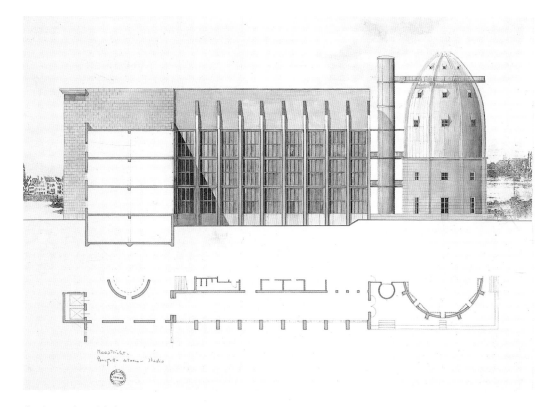

BONNEFANTEN MUSEUM
Maastricht, the Netherlands
1990–95

Section and partial plan

Zinc-clad dome tops café and other museum spaces

Main entrance to the museum. At right is a former ceramics studio that has been restored and is now part of the museum

Aerial view of the complex

1991

Robert Venturi

MIELPARQUE NIKKO KIRIFURI RESORT
Nikko National Park,
Tochigi Prefecture, Japan
1992–97

Venturi, Scott Brown, and Associates, Ltd., Architects, in association with Marunouchi Architects and Engineers and Andropogon Associates, Inc.

In 1992 the Japanese Ministry of Posts and Telecommunications commissioned VSBA to design a hotel complex adjacent to Nikko National Park, where centuries-old Buddhist and Shinto shrines are located. The recently completed Mielparque Nikko Kirifuri Resort includes a ninety-seven-room hotel and conference center, tennis courts, and a spa and swimming facility.

Throughout the complex, building proportions and facades suggest traditional rural architecture: the ornamental roof structures symbolize vernacular roof forms and overhangs, and the wall appliqué pattern alludes to exposed frame construction. The main hotel, a series of linked buildings, recedes into the mountainous wooded setting. Together the elements present the resort as a modern, streamlined version of the ancient Japanese village.

A bridge spans the ravine at the approach to the hotel. Because it is perpendicular to the toll road and visible from it, this structure was designed as a sign to identify the complex and enrich its image. Its form is juxtaposed with its reinforced-concrete structure, which is derived from contemporary engineering technology; a decorative plane on each face represents a symbolic abstraction of a traditional Japanese bridge. The planes are made of corrugated aluminum whose light color is recessive within the natural setting.

The hotel complex is designed to be perceived from the exterior as a series of modest buildings suggesting a rural village. In contrast, the resort's interiors appear innovative and contemporary. The large spa facility is ornamented with giant green and yellow aluminum tree

View of the bridge and hotel

The village street in the hotel

leaves that refer to the complex's verdant surroundings. The dominant element of the hotel's interior is a pedestrian "village street" punctuated with colorful, abstracted signs and murals depicting historical and contemporary motifs. These symbols celebrate the traditions and spirit of Japanese urban and village life. Restaurants, cafés, and retail areas line this street, making it a lively place for both adults and children. To the east rise six stories of hotel facilities, and to the west are located conference rooms, lobbies, underground parking, and tennis courts. Similar architectural elements and identical materials are employed on the hotel complex and spa facility facades to promote unity within the whole. Each building is essentially generic in its expression, and through the use of subtle allusion a sense of drama is added.

The Nikko Kirifuri Resort also fuses Japanese and American environmental design. Central cogeneration and wastewater treatment plants conserve energy and reduce negative environmental impact. The storm-water retention system forms appealing ponds. Natural ventilation is used throughout the guest rooms and common spaces, enhancing indoor air quality and reducing air conditioning requirements. Hundreds of native trees and shrubs dug from the construction site have been stored for later replanting.

Preliminary sketch for the village street

Spa building, south facade

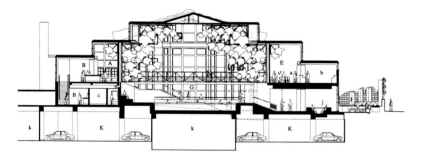

Section, spa building

Spa pool

VANNA VENTURI HOUSE
Chestnut Hill,
Philadelphia, Pennsylvania
1962–64

**Robert Venturi with
Arthur Jones**

Main facade

Dining room

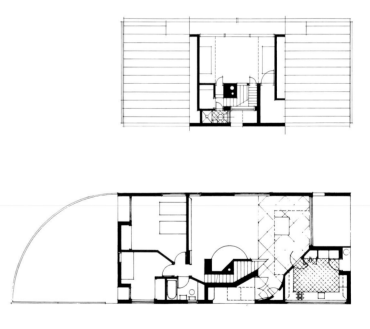

Plans, second and first floors

GORDON WU HALL
Butler College, Princeton
University, New Jersey
1980–83

Venturi, Scott Brown, and
Associates, Ltd., Architects

Hall houses a dormitory and dining facilities

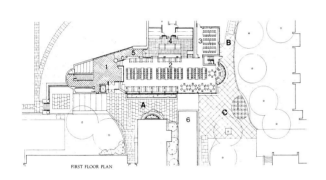

Plan, first floor

Sketch of east elevation

Dining/lounge area

Aerial view

1992

Alvaro Siza

GALICIAN CENTER FOR CONTEMPORARY ART
Santiago de Compostela, Spain
1988–93

The museum, commissioned by the regional government of Galicia, stands within the grounds of an old convent in the city of Santiago de Compostela, in northwest Spain. The museum looks toward the entrance of the Church of Santo Domingo while redefining the limits of the old garden by integrating them into the project. The varied, ascending, asymmetric levels of the garden also echo the geometry of the new museum and form a natural transition between the sloping site and the street. The urban and architectural strategy for the museum seeks to define a space that more coherently relates the existing buildings of the area and reorganizes a previously degraded area of the city.

The compact three-story museum building is composed of two elongated wings that form a V shape. The intersection of these two wings defines a triangular atrium that extends the full height of the museum and houses the stairs leading to the exhibition galleries. The circulation route through the galleries culminates in a roof terrace for sculpture exhibitions and a ramp leading to a platform overlooking the convent and the city.

The granite cladding of the exterior, with its subtle variations in color, refers to traditional building materials of the area. In contrast to the closed exterior, the luminous interior is finished in white marble and stucco in the atrium and circulation spaces, and oak flooring in the exhibition spaces. The upper galleries are top-lit by central openings, and suspended diffusers protect the artwork from direct sunlight.

Entrance

The museum in its urban context

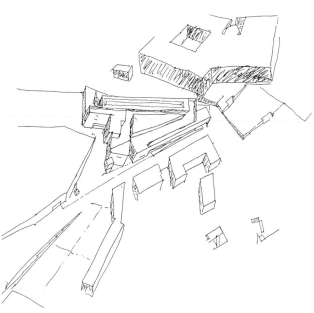

Preliminary sketch

Museum with the Church of Santo Domingo in the background

Lobby

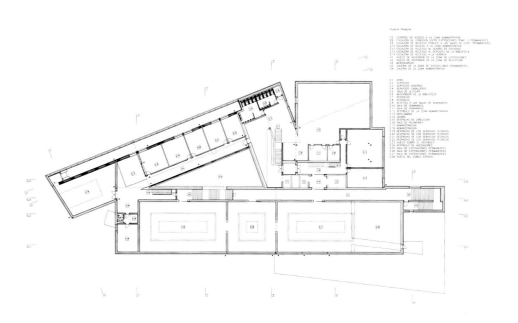

Plan, second floor

Partial view of the courtyard porch

Vestibule

**TEACHER TRAINING
COLLEGE
Setubal, Portugal
1986–94**

Courtyard between two wings of the college

SCHOOL OF ARCHITECTURE
Oporto, Portugal
1987–93

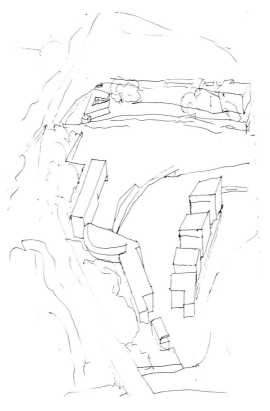

Preliminary sketch

Site plan

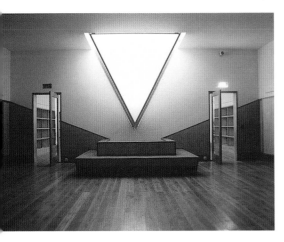

Library

Classroom buildings

Preliminary sketch

Jury Citation
Fumihiko Maki of Japan is an architect whose work is intelligent and artistic in concept and expression, meticulously achieved. He is a modernist who has fused the best of both Eastern and Western cultures to create an architecture representing the age-old qualities of his native country while juxtaposing contemporary construction methods and materials.

Early in his career, he was a founding member of an avant-garde group of young Japanese architects calling themselves Metabolists, changeability and flexibility being key elements of their view. One aim was never to design in isolation from the city structure as a whole. Maki has expressed his constant concern for the "parts" and the "whole," describing one of his goals as achieving a dynamic equilibrium that includes sometimes conflicting masses, volumes, and materials.

He uses light in a masterful way, making it as tangible a part of every design as are the walls and roof. In each building he searches for a means of making transparency, translucency, and opacity exist in total harmony. To echo his own words, "Detailing is what gives architecture its rhythm and scale."

There is amazing diversity in Maki's work – from the awesome Nippon Convention Center near Tokyo, with its man-made mountain range of stainless steel roofs, to his earlier and smaller YKK Guest House or planned orphan village in Poland.

The dimensions of his work measure a career that has greatly enriched architecture. As a prolific author as well as architect and teacher, Maki contributes significantly to the understanding of the profession.

Fumihiko Maki

KAZE-NO-OKA CREMATORIUM
Nakatsu, Oita Prefecture, Japan 1993–97

The Kaze-no-Oka Crematorium is located in Nakatsu, in southern Japan. On part of the site, ancient burial mounds have been discovered and incorporated into the surrounding public park. Seen from the park, the crematorium appears as a partially submerged earthwork, a few fragments of which are free-standing sculptural forms that create an abstract landscape. The focus of the park is an elliptical field that dips at the center to form a basin; there, as one descends, the surrounding landscape disappears from view, creating a place embraced by the earth.

The crematorium itself comprises three distinct zones, which are loosely connected – a ceremonial area, where funerals are held; a waiting area for the family and friends of the deceased; and a cremation area, where final respects are offered. From the point of arrival at the porte cochere, the path of movement is prolonged to heighten the ritualistic experience of transition and establish a tranquil environment.

Throughout the building natural light plays a critical role; carefully emitted and controlled by a variety of means, it helps define the mood of each particular space. One passes ritualistically from space to space in the crematorium. At the entrance is an open-air porch with a column that is symbolically illuminated from the sky. In the oratory and enshrinement room, light enters from the upper side walls, and its intensity is softened and filtered by vertical louvers. The cremation area is arrayed around an interior courtyard with a reflecting pool. Here outside vistas have been limited to focus one's awareness inward. The effect of light is dramatized by the reflection of the water cast on the concrete walls. The waiting room is the only vertical space

Enshrinement room

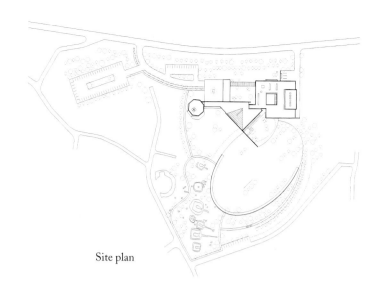

Site plan

View from the south of the octagonal chapel and buildings housing the waiting and cremation areas

in the sequence, and its effect is accentuated by a double-height column, a sweeping curved soffit, and a large skylight. Completing the sequence is the chapel, an octagonal space with three sources of light – a horizontal and a vertical glazed band, and glazed circular openings in the ceiling – whose sizes have been limited to control the effects of the light and further enhance one's appreciation of it.

The building is constructed of wood, concrete, Cor-Ten steel, brick, and slate. An ensemble of elemental materials and natural light, the Kaze-no-Oka Crematorium is a place of serenity and dignity in which to pay a final farewell.

Waiting area and staircase

Walkway around the courtyard

Chapel

Entrance to the cremation area

Keel arch of the main stadium

MUNICIPAL GYMNASIUM
Fujisawa, Kanagawa
Prefecture, Japan
1980–84

Main stadium

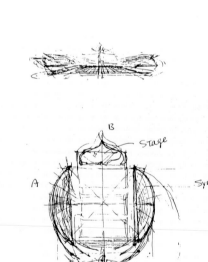

Preliminary sketch

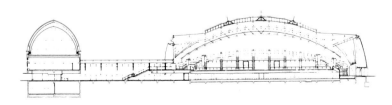

Section through the small stadium, entrance hall, and main stadium

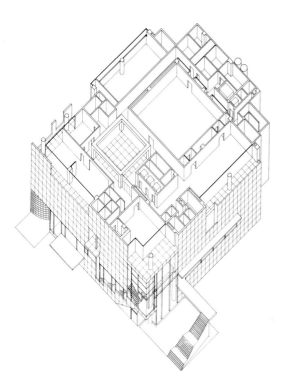

Cutaway axonometric drawing through the fourth floor

South facade

TEPIA SCIENCE PAVILION
Tokyo, Japan
1983–89

View toward the outdoors from the lobby

West Building, student lounge

Jury Citation

Christian de Portzamparc's new architecture is of our time, bound by neither classicism nor modernism. His expanded perceptions and ideas seek answers beyond mere style. It is a new architecture characterized by seeing buildings – their functions and the life within them – in ways that require wide-ranging but thoughtful exploration for unprecedented solutions.

Every architect who aspires to greatness must in some sense reinvent architecture; conceive new solutions; develop a special design character; find a new aesthetic vocabulary. Portzamparc's work exhibits all these characteristics. He has an unusually clear and consistent vision, devising highly original spaces that serve a variety of functions – on an urban scale in the Cité de la Musique, or on a more personal, individual scale in a housing project or the delightfully chic Café Beaubourg. He is a gifted composer using space, structure, texture, form, light, and color – all shaped by his own vision. This reinvented architecture, no matter how idiosyncratic or original, still has its common source in modernism, appropriately assimilated.

Portzamparc is a prominent member of a new generation of French architects who have incorporated the lessons of the Beaux-Arts into an exuberant collage of contemporary architectural idioms, at once bold, colorful, and original. His is an architecture that draws on French cultural tradition while paying homage to his countryman, the master architect Le Corbusier. It is a lyrical architecture that takes great risks and evokes excitement in its audience. Portzamparc is a high-wire artist with sure and confident footwork.

1994 Christian de Portzamparc

CITÉ DE LA MUSIQUE
Paris, France
1984–95

Located near the south entrance to the park of La Villette, the Cité de la Musique is composed of two complementary yet highly differentiated buildings that face each other on either side of the Great Hall. To the west is the conservatory of music; to the east a structure housing a concert hall, a museum of music, rehearsal rooms, and administrative offices. The whole forms a unique complex devoted to music and dance and to extending the sphere of influence of France's National Conservatory.

The West Building has a curved and stepped white facade that appears to float above the reflecting pool in front of it. This block is sited along Avenue Jean-Jaurès. The freer East Building takes the form of a large triangle and is open to the park.

From the first, the design undermined the axis of the Great Hall and created a dissymmetry to play down the emphatic nature of this approach to the park. Together the two buildings define a vast triangle extending the static axis of the Great Hall and opening out onto the dynamic axis of the park with its distant view of the Geode theater. The West and East Buildings, the Great Hall, the park and its follies are thereby all linked.

The interiors of the Cité de la Musique obey a single principle: the opaque volumes, which are highly differentiated in form and size, are bound together by transparent volumes, fissures of light that work as interstitial fabric. The circulation and meeting points are either completely of glass or open-air. Thus despite the density of the program, light and views are omnipresent.

The Cité de la Musique is a living, fluid, complex place, whose architecture can be "traveled" in a single sweeping glance. It is precisely this sequencing, with its durations, discontinuities, and happy discoveries, that makes the architecture a musical event. Architecture is here an art of movement, devoted to sound.

West Building, main facade

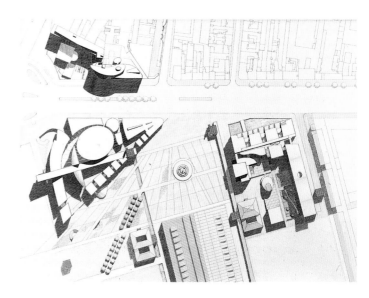

Site plan, East and West Buildings

West Building, inner courtyard and garden of conservatory

West Building, student residence (left) and organ hall (right)

East Building, main entrance

East Building, panoramic view

East Building, concert hall

Foyer around the concert hall

East Building, perspective section

LES HAUTES FORMES
HOUSING
Paris, France
1975–79

View from one end of the complex along the rue des Hautes Formes

Housing and courtyard

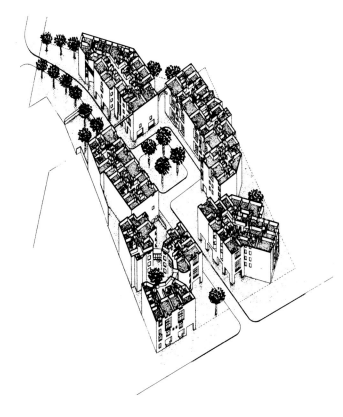

Cutaway axonometric drawing

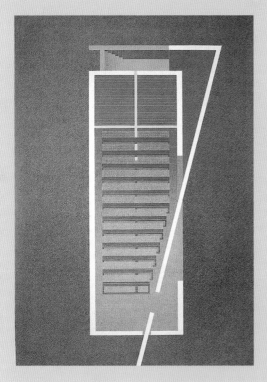

Rendering of plan

Jury Citation

At an age when most architects are beginning to design their first serious works, Ando has accomplished an extraordinary oeuvre, primarily in his native Japan, that already sets him apart. Working with smooth-as-silk concrete, he creates spaces using walls, which he defines as the most basic element of architecture, but also the most enriching. In spite of his consistent use of materials and the elements of pillar, wall, and vault, his different combinations of them always prove exciting and dynamic. Ando's design concepts and materials have linked international modernism to the Japanese aesthetic tradition. His dedication to and understanding of the importance of craftsmanship have earned him the appellation of builder as well as architect.

Ando is accomplishing his self-imposed mission to restore the unity between house and nature. Using the most basic geometric forms, he creates microcosms for the individual with ever-changing patterns of light.

The Pritzker Architecture Prize honors Tadao Ando not only for works completed but also for future projects that when realized will most certainly further enrich the art of architecture.

1995
Tadao Ando

CHURCH OF THE LIGHT
Ibaraki, Osaka Prefecture, Japan
1987–89

The Church of the Light is a freestanding addition to an existing wood church and parsonage located in a quiet residential suburb of Osaka. It consists of a rectangular volume sliced through at a fifteen-degree angle by a freestanding wall, which serves to divide the entrance from the chapel area itself. This indirect access to the chapel emphasizes one's movement across the threshold between the outside and the sacred interior space.

The floors and pews are fabricated from low-cost reclaimed scaffolding planks, which, with their rough-textured surface, emphasize the simple and honest character of the space. The floor inside the chapel descends in stages toward the altar. This represents one of the most important concepts in Ando's design of the church: the expression of the equality between the worshippers and the pastor. The pastor thus preaches from an area below, rather than the more conventional position above, the congregation.

Light penetrates the profound darkness of this box through a cross cut into the altar wall. The introspective and closed interior of the chapel is intensely focused on this cross of light. Ando intentionally limited the number of apertures since light displays its brilliance only against a backdrop of darkness. The presence of nature in the chapel is confined to this element of light, and it is thereby rendered extremely abstract. In response to this abstraction, the architecture is made continually more pure. A linear pattern is drawn on the floor by rays of sun, and at night by the moonlight – and the congregation is enveloped in a cross of light. With the passage of time and the change of seasons, the cross of light identifies the relationship between man and nature in its purest form.

Sanctuary during worship

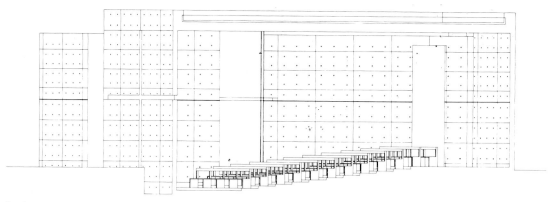

Section

Now, almost ten years after the completion of the Church of the Light in 1989, Ando has been given the opportunity to replace the existing wood church as well, thus offering it a chance to be reborn. The new church will house a Sunday school and meeting place. Ando is presently in the process of preparing the schematics for this extension. He always aspires to create a unified totality in his architecture. Accordingly, the central theme of this project became how to tie a new structure to the already completed form. With the second addition, he aims to bring a new totality to the Church of the Light without sacrificing its initial power.

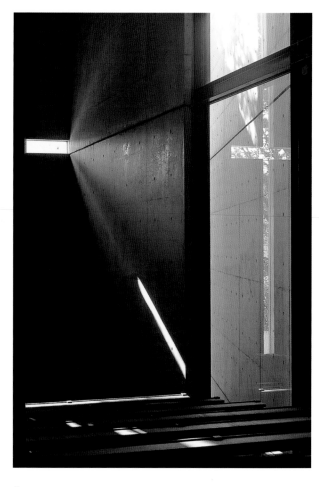

Sanctuary

Sanctuary entrance

Detail of the pews and floor

Aerial view of the house and addition

Living room

South facade

Aerial view

Stepped roof/plaza

**CHIKATSU-ASUKA
HISTORICAL MUSEUM
Osaka, Japan
1990–94**

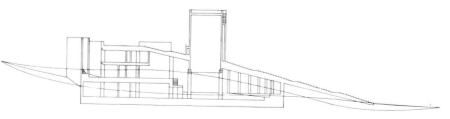

Section

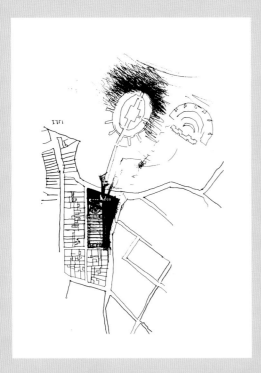
Sketch of site plan

Jury Citation
José Rafael Moneo is above all an architect of tremendous range. His flexibility in varying the appearance of his works based on their differing contexts is reflected in the way he takes on each new commission as a fresh exercise. He draws on an incredible reservoir of concepts and ideas, which he filters through the specifics of the site, the purpose, the form, the climate, and other circumstances of the project. As a result, each of his buildings is unique, but at the same time, uniquely recognizable as being from his palette.

That palette has ranged from the ancient, in the Museum of Roman Art in Mérida, to the minimalist, in the Kursaal Auditorium and Congress Center planned for San Sebastián. There are infinite variations between these two examples, embodied in everything from residences to art museums, a railway station, an airport, a factory, a hotel, banks, and other office buildings. Each of his designs has a confident and timeless quality indicative of a master architect whose talent is obvious from the first concept to the last detail of the completed building. He regards the materials and techniques of construction to be just as important as the architect's vision and concept.

As a writer, critic, and teacher, he devotes almost as much time to education as he does to design, and further shapes the future of architecture with his words.

Moneo's career is the ideal example of knowledge and experience enhancing the mutual interaction of theory, practice, and teaching. We honor Moneo for these parallel efforts of the past, present, and future.

1996

José Rafael Moneo

NATIONAL MUSEUM OF ROMAN ART
Mérida, Spain
1980–85

Founded by legionaries of Augustus in 24 B.C., Mérida became the most important Roman city in Spain by the fall of the empire. Almost completely destroyed after the Muslim invasion, it began to recover under Arab rule. It has endured through the centuries, and today is a modest rural town in the province of Extremadura.

Archaeological excavations were begun in the late nineteenth century, and numerous monuments, statues, and other artifacts have been recovered. Today the theater and arena are impressive reminders of the town's past. Not far from these monumental relics is the National Museum of Roman Art, which is constructed over a still-buried portion of the Roman town.

The primary goal was to build a museum that would offer people an opportunity to understand aspects of the town's Roman heritage. Without falling into a strict imitation of Roman architecture,

Moneo adopted the Roman construction system – massive masonry-bearing walls filled with concrete. Other Roman building techniques, materials, and proportions were utilized as well, and prominence was given to construction as an expression of architecture itself. The materiality of the Roman brick wall becomes, finally, the most important feature in the architecture of the museum.

The main exhibition hall is traversed by a series of parallel walls that have been opened with towering arches. The perspective view through the arches reveals the scale of the building and expresses the continuity of the space therein. These walls also define lateral bays for the display of some of the most valuable pieces in the museum's collection. The walls function as partitions, on which are hung cornices, capitals, mosaics, and fragments of statuary. These surfaces are not con-

Main exhibition hall

Aerial view

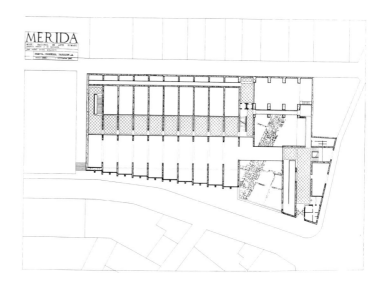

Plan, second floor, showing walkways

sidered to be mere neutral supports for the objects; rather, the translucent white marble of the relics may be seen in a dialectical interplay with the material presence of the brick walls. Natural light, another fundamental concern in the museum's design, enters through sky-lights above and windows set high in the facades. The constantly changing intensity and color of the light contributes to the dialogue between the works of art and the building itself.

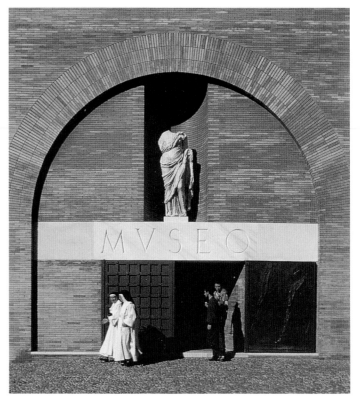

Entrance

Second-floor walkway

Sketches of elevations and plan

Roman ruins in the lower level

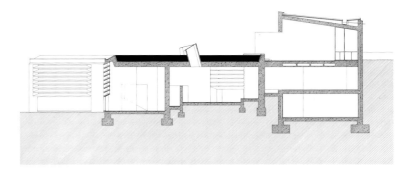

Section

Panoramic view

PILAR AND JOAN MIRÓ
FOUNDATION
Palma de Mallorca, Spain
1987–92

View of a gallery, with the entry porch and roof pool

Aerial view

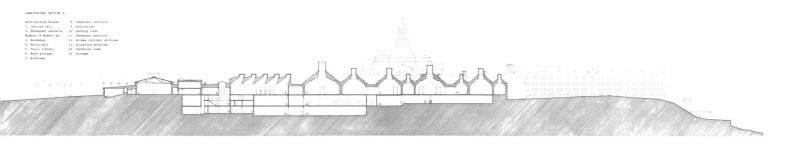

LONGITUDINAL SECTION A

Architecture Museum   8. Temporary exhibits
1. Lecture hall   9. Auditorium
2. Permanent exhibits   10. Packing room
Museum of Modern Art   11. Permanent exhibits
3. Bookshop   12. Access corridor archives
4. Entry hall   13. Sculpture archives
5. Photo library   14. Technical room
6. Book storage   15. Storage
7. Archives

Section

**MUSEUMS OF MODERN
ART AND ARCHITECTURE**
Stockholm, Sweden
1991–97

Gallery

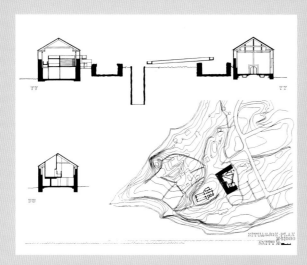

Sections and site plan

Sverre Fehn

Jury Citation
The architecture of Norwegian Sverre Fehn is a fascinating and exciting combination of modern forms tempered by the Scandinavian tradition and culture from which it springs. He gives great primacy in his designs to the relationship between the built and the natural environment.

The Norwegian Pavilion at the 1958 World's Fair in Brussels gave early notice of his special talents. The Nordic Pavilion at the Venice Biennale a few years later was a confirmation. Since then, Fehn has proven that he is an architect with many dimensions, as comfortable with the design of furniture, exhibitions, and objects as with buildings. His eloquence with materials is easily matched by his poetic command of words.

He has avoided fads and fashions that have influenced much of contemporary architecture, patiently evolving his own individual style, always seeking improvement.

He has broken new ground in giving modern architectural form to elements of his native Norwegian landscape – northern light, gray stone, and verdant forest – blending fantasy and reality into buildings that are both contemporary and timeless.

ARCHBISHOPRIC MUSEUM
Hamar, Norway
1967–79

In his scheme for the Archbishopric Museum of Hamar, located in an area of great archaeological interest, Fehn made use of the remains of a farm structure dating from the early nineteenth century. The rural building rests on top of the ruins of a medieval fortress that was demolished in the second half of the sixteenth century and traces of which are still visible. The site is particularly important because it lies along the Kaupang Trail, the route that the bishop of Hamar followed on his way to Rome in 1302.

The museum was intended to house the artifacts recovered in the excavation of the site, to permit the dig to continue, and to provide a series of exhibition rooms for displays on peasant life. Above the old stone wall are wooden structures painted a rust color and covered by a double-pitched roof made of clay tiles alternating with glass tiles, which allow light to penetrate into the museum. In the courtyard, above the ruins of the old fortress, a long exposed-concrete ramp leads directly from the excavation site to the corner of the upper story between the conference room, restrooms, and museum hallway.

The museum engages in a continual dialogue between exterior and interior. The displays unfold like a story or a series of voyages to different points in history. Exhibition spaces and resting areas are linked by a long path across ramps and terraces, through visible and evoked memories of local history. The light that filters through the roof blends with the light that enters through the openings in the old wall, which have been not filled but merely covered with unframed glass. In displays of extreme simplicity, the objects are exhibited on rudimentary iron supports that not only establish the sequence for studying the artifacts but also form a sort of artificial passageway to attract the attention of the public.

A spiral stair and ramp connect the two levels of the museum

Partial view of the exterior from the courtyard

Overall view of the courtyard

Auditorium wing

View toward the excavation area under the museum

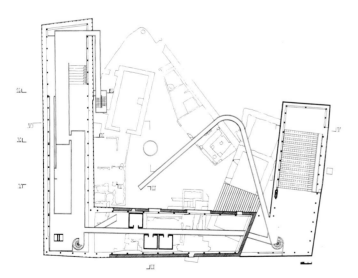

Plan, first floor

Ramp connecting the two levels of the museum

GLACIER MUSEUM
Fjaerland, Norway
1989–91

Side view, with main entrance canopy at left

Main entrance and adjacent stair leading to the roof terrace

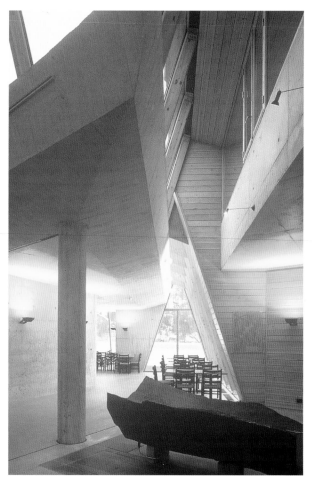

Restaurant

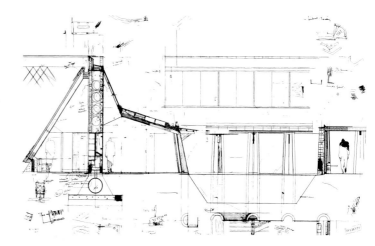

Study for section

AUKRUST MUSEUM OF
DRAWINGS
Alvdal, Norway
1993–96

Main facade and entrance

Rear facade

View of the angled roofs of the cases

1998

Renzo Piano

JEAN-MARIE TJIBAOU CULTURAL CENTER
Nouméa, New Caledonia
1991–98

Renzo Piano Building Workshop

A series of cases, as Piano calls them, curving structures made of wooden ribs and slats and inspired by traditional building crafts of the island, forms the new cultural center in Nouméa. The result of an invited international competition, the center has been donated by the French government to its overseas department and the people of New Caledonia. With its exhibition spaces, auditorium, library, and amphitheater it will commemorate traditional Kanak culture and provide a focus for its evolution.

The center is arranged in three villages or clusters of cases linked by a covered promenade. The first houses the reception area and exhibitions. It is the largest case and is devoted to the history of the Kanaks. The middle village contains two levels of offices for the center's staff. The third village features a conference room, video center, and library.

The design is the result of inspiration from two distinct sources: traditional building materials and techniques, and sophisticated technology. The cases are constructed of a double layer of laminated timber ribs, which are connected by a horseshoe-shaped steel beam. Each one has a sloping roof whose frame is stiffened by tension cables. A system of louvers provides climate control. By adjusting the lower louvers, natural ventilation is manipulated to maintain a comfortable temperature inside. The striking imagery of the center is a response to the topography and vegetation of the site. Visually the cases dominate the design and rise on the central ridge of a peninsula, yet they are akin to the large pines and palms surrounding the center. Although they are not replicas of local structures, they evoke the traditional Kanak huts by their organization in clusters.

Partial view of the center with traditional Kanak huts in the foreground

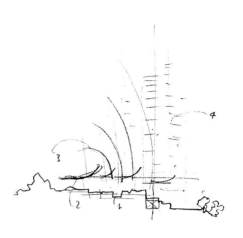

Preliminary sketch

Aerial view

View across the bay

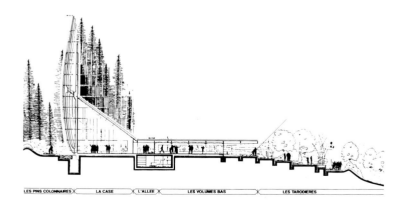

Section of the first village, which houses the entry, exhibition, and cafeteria areas

Detail of the ribs of a case

Library

Auditorium

View from the east

NATIONAL CENTER FOR SCIENCE AND TECHNOLOGY
Amsterdam, the Netherlands
1992–97

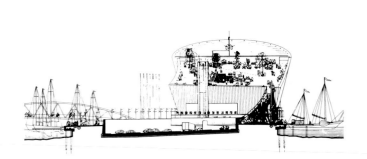

South elevation with section through the tunnel

System of stairways links several levels of exhibition spaces and visitor services

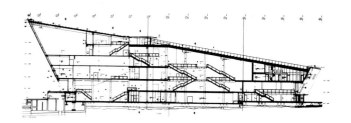

Section

View into the south end of the building

BEYELER FOUNDATION
Riehen, Basel, Switzerland
1993–97

West facade

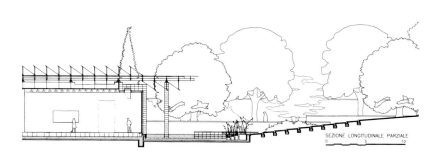

Partial section

Detail of the roof and reflecting pool

The Pritzker Architecture Prize Jurors and Administrators

1979–present	J. Carter Brown, Chairman of the Jury
1988–present	Bill N. Lacy, Executive Director
1979–82	Lord Clark of Saltwood
1979–82	Cesar Pelli
1979–84	Arata Isozaki
1979–84	J. Irwin Miller
1981–85	Philip Johnson
1982–86	Thomas J. Watson, Jr.
1983–91	Kevin Roche
1984–present	Giovanni Agnelli
1985–88	Fumihiko Maki
1985–93	Ricardo Legorreta
1987–present	Ada Louise Huxtable
1987–present	Lord Rothschild
1991–present	Toshio Nakamura
1993–95	Frank O. Gehry
1993–98	Charles Correa
1996–present	Jorge Silvetti
1979–84	Carleton Smith, Secretary to the Jury
1979–86	Arthur Drexler, Consultant to the Jury
1985–87	Brendan Gill, Secretary to the Jury
1987–88	Stuart Wrede, Acting Consultant to the Jury

Biographies of the Architects

Tadao Ando

Tadao Ando's design approach combines Japanese aesthetic traditions with international modernism and is intimately tied to the natural environment. His goal is to ensure "a place for the individual, a zone for oneself within society."[1]

Ando was born in Osaka in 1941. His interest in architecture grew from a childhood fascination with the woodworking craft. As a young man he served as a carpenter's apprentice and worked with others in the fields of design and city planning. He continued his self-education, reading extensively and traveling abroad to study the works of Le Corbusier, Ludwig Mies van der Rohe, Alvar Aalto, Frank Lloyd Wright, and Louis Kahn. Le Corbusier's Unité d'Habitation in Marseilles first sparked Ando's interest in the use of concrete. The thick, smooth concrete walls of his buildings have become one of his trademarks.

Ando's architectural vocabulary is subtle and minimalist. It relies on a simple composition of geometric forms with diverse spaces dramatized by light. Impervious to current movements or schools, his work reflects a consistent adherence to a personal philosophy. He gained recognition with one of his first commissions, Azuma House, a small row house in Osaka completed in 1976. Its sheer unadorned wall of exposed concrete encloses a courtyard, creating a tranquil space in touch with nature, "physically and psychologically isolating [the urban dweller] from the outside world."

The Rokko Housing Complex (Phase I, 1978–83; Phase II, 1985–93), embedded in a hillside overlooking Osaka Bay, is designed as a cluster of exposed-concrete units. Their strong geometry contrasts sharply with the natural surroundings. The complex features various appealing public spaces that serve as gathering places for the residents. The project exemplifies the confrontation between Eastern and Western values that characterizes Ando's architecture. He regards it as one of his most important works, and plans have been proposed for Phase III.

One of the most celebrated of his ecclesiastical projects, the Church on the Water, in Tomamu, Hokkaido Prefecture (1985–88), lives up to his creed, "It would best suit me to build houses without roofs – then nature would remain palpable."

Ando has taught and lectured at leading institutions in the United States and abroad. He has received numerous awards in recognition of his extraordinary body of work, including the Gold Medal of the French Academy of Architecture (1989), the Carlsberg Architectural Prize (1992), the Pritzker Prize (1995), and the Praemium Imperiale (1996). He has been designated an honorary fellow by architectural organizations in Germany, the United States, and Great Britain.

1. Mirko Zardini, ed., *Rokko Housing*, Quaderni di Casabella series (Milan: Electa, Nov. 1986), p. 17.

Luis Barragán

Luis Barragán was awarded the Pritzker Prize in 1980 for work described as "a sublime act of the poetic imagination."[1] Master of what he himself called "emotional architecture," the sources of his inspiration are found in the whitewashed walls, serene courtyards, and brightly colored streets of Mexico and the villages of North Africa and Spain.

Barragán was born in 1902 in Guadalajara, Mexico, and received his professional degree in engineering there at age twenty-three. In the late 1920s he was associated with a movement known as the Escuela Tapatía or Guadalajara School, which espoused a theory of architecture dedicated to the vigorous adherence to regional traditions. Most of Barragán's early work was carried out in Guadalajara and concentrated on private houses and residential subdivisions. In them he blended the traditional crafts of the region – mosaics, glazed tiles, wrought-iron grillwork – with bold colors to give dimension to a particular space. Inside, light is filtered through translucent panes of colored glass. Influenced greatly by French writer and landscape architect Ferdinand Bac, Barragán focused on the close relationship between landscape, color, and architecture. The Efraín Gonzáles Luna House, built in 1929, is an early manifestation of his mature style.

In 1936 Barragán moved to Mexico City and designed several small houses and apartment buildings that emphasized practicality and modernity, in keeping with the time.

After 1940 he devoted himself to the planning of large urban developments, including El Pedragal de San Ángel, Mexico. The convent and chapel of the Capuchinas Sacramentarias, completed in 1955, remains one of the great successes of his career. In 1984 Barragán was made an honorary member of the American Academy of Arts and Letters. He died in 1988 in Mexico City.

1. Jury Citation, *The Pritzker Architecture Prize, 1980: Luis Barragán* (Los Angeles: Hyatt Foundation, 1980).

Gottfried Böhm

Born in 1920 in Offenbach-am-Main, Germany, Gottfried Böhm is a member of a family of architects spanning several generations, one whose work has reflected the solidity and substance appropriate to its many commissions for churches and civic, judicial, and cultural buildings.

Böhm trained in Munich in both architecture and sculpture from 1942 to 1947 and worked with his father, Dominikus, the leading architect of Catholic churches in the interwar period. Gottfried took over the office after his father's death in 1955, completing a series of projects that arrived at structural and spatial innovations only dreamed of by the Expressionist generation of the senior Böhm.

Since the beginning of his career Böhm's respect for history – its preservation and creative extension – has been evident in his work. In one of his most outstanding early designs, the Bensberg Town Hall (1962–67), the council chamber and administrative offices are planted among the ruins of a medieval castle and, further juxtaposing the old with the new, crowned by a multi-faceted concrete tower that engages in a dialogue with the old castle of Bensberg. The Church of the Pilgrimage at Neviges, Germany (1960–64), is his best-known building; with its mysterious soaring interior and long ceremonial approach, it has been acclaimed as one of the great religious monuments of the twentieth century.

Böhm's work has changed with the times. He became increasingly interested in issues of urban planning and the connection between public and private space. After the early 1970s, steel and glass replaced freeform concrete, which he had used as a sculptural building material. The types of buildings he designed also changed, with town halls and commercial buildings outnumbering churches. Of these projects perhaps the best known is the Civic Center in Bergisch-Gladbach (1977–80).

Böhm has conducted seminars at the Massachusetts Institute of Technology and the University of Pennsylvania, but his architecture is relatively unknown in America. He was awarded the Gold Medal of the French Academy of Architecture in 1982, and was made an honorary fellow of the AIA in the same year. The 1986 Pritzker Prize brought much-deserved recognition to his unique oeuvre.

Gordon Bunshaft

In 1988 the tenth Pritzker Prize was awarded to two masters of modernism, Gordon Bunshaft of the United States and Oscar Niemeyer of Brazil.

Bunshaft was born in Buffalo, New York, in 1909. He received his bachelor's and master's degrees in architecture from the Massachusetts Institute of Technology.

As design partner of the New York office of Skidmore, Owings, and Merrill during the 1950s, Bunshaft shaped most of the firm's major work and, with his devotion to the uncluttered glass-and-steel tradition of Ludwig Mies van der Rohe, made Miesian architecture a symbol of financial integrity. His design for Lever House in New York (1947–52), the first of many prestigious commissions for corporate headquarters, pioneered the curtain-walled slab structures that would rise worldwide. Bunshaft's understanding of contemporary technology was unsurpassed. His glass-and-steel structures exploited America's production-line economy and made a design asset of prefabrication. He believed that architects should press manufacturers to experiment with a great variety of products and from these try to evolve new building solutions.

Bunshaft's illustrious contributions to the urban/corporate world include such diverse projects as the Beinecke Rare Book and Manuscript Library at Yale University (1960–63), the Hirshhorn Museum and Sculpture Garden, Washington, D.C. (1966–74), and the National Commercial Bank in Jeddah, Saudi Arabia (1978–84).

Bunshaft received the Brunner Prize in Architecture from the American Academy and Institute of Arts and Letters in 1955 and its Gold Medal in 1984. He died at the age of eighty-one in 1990, ending an architectural career that spanned forty years.

Sverre Fehn

Although he came of age in the shadow of modernism and acknowledges its importance, Sverre Fehn has a strong relationship to his origins. He was born in Kongsberg, Norway, in 1924, and received his degree from the Architectural School of Oslo in 1949. With other Norwegian architects of the same generation he formed the Norwegian branch of CIAM (Congrès International d'Architecture Moderne) called PAGON (Progressive Architects Group Oslo Norway). The group created a new architecture based on the modern movement but expressed in a regional form, both in its choice of materials and language. Important to Fehn's architectural development were his travels to North Africa in the early 1950s and his tenure with architect and designer Jean Prouvé in Paris in 1953–54.

With one of his first commissions, the Norwegian Pavilion for the 1958 World Exhibition in Brussels, Fehn displayed one of the most essential characteristics of his architecture – the expressive representation of its elements through structure and material. With a restricted palette of wood, glass, and concrete the pavilion expressed the simple honesty that epitomizes Fehn's work. The roof, which projects over the main facade, indicates the entrance. The play of light through the large sliding-glass panels unites exterior and interior. Fehn considers light to be another material of construction. His projects conform to the order of the landscape. "Any act of building is an assault on nature," he says, and he strives to create structures that allow the observer to see the beauty in materialized construction – the language of architecture – integrated with the beauty of the natural setting.

Fehn has built a variety of types of structures, from single-family houses to restaurants to civic buildings. He is perhaps best known for his museums, such as the Hedmark Cathedral Museum or Archbishopric Museum in Hamar (1967–79), the Glacier Museum in Fjaerland (1989–91), and the Aukrust Museum of Drawings in Alvdal (1993–96), which reflect his continuing exploration of new frontiers in architectural expression.

Fehn was professor of architecture at his alma mater in Oslo from 1971 until 1995 and has lectured extensively in Scandinavia and abroad. He is an honorary member of the RIBA, the AIA, the Swedish Royal Academy, and the Royal Academy of Arts of Copenhagen. He was awarded the Pritzker Prize in 1997.

Frank O. Gehry

The Guggenheim Museum in Bilbao, Spain, which opened in October 1997, has been hailed as a masterpiece – the crowning achievement of California's irrepressible Frank O. Gehry. Recipient of the 1989 Pritzker Prize, Gehry is considered by a number of critics and even some fellow practitioners to be one of the most original architects working today.

Gehry was born in Canada in 1929 and

moved to California in 1947. After putting himself through architecture school at the University of Southern California, from which he graduated in 1954 at the top of his class, he spent a year at Harvard, studying city planning and auditing courses in other fields that interested him – music and art, politics, sociology, and philosophy. In 1962, after three years with the Los Angeles firm of Victor Gruen Associates and a year in Paris, Gehry established his own practice.

In the 1970s Gehry began actively to pursue his interest in the relationship between painting, sculpture, and architecture. His unique style, described by critics as his "builder's mode," is epitomized in the design for his own house in Santa Monica (1978–79). Gehry "wrapped" the pink shingled, 1920s two-story Dutch Colonial he called "a dumb little house" in an outer wall of corrugated aluminum topped by chain-link fencing and punctuated by asymmetrical windows that reveal the studs and bracing of the interior. The project expressed Gehry's belief that houses look more beautiful when they are being built than when they are finished.

This turning point in Gehry's career led to an increasingly sculptural approach to architecture. In his projects for the California Aerospace Museum, Los Angeles (1982–84), and the Winton Guest House, Wayzata, Minnesota (1983–86), he introduced his concept of a "village of forms" – the notion of breaking down the structure into discrete, dissimilar forms – which he would develop further in many subsequent projects.

During the 1980s and 1990s Gehry's commissions grew in scale and importance. Projects completed during this period include the Yale Psychiatric Institute, New Haven (1985–86), the Vitra International Furniture Manufacturing Facility and Museum in Weil-am-Rhein, Germany (1986–96), and the Frederick R. Weisman Art Museum in Minneapolis.

In 1986 the first retrospective of Gehry's work was organized by the Walker Art Center in Minneapolis; it included not only architecture but also his furniture designs. Gehry has received worldwide recognition

and awards, including the Praemium Imperiale in 1992 and, in 1994, the first Lillian Gish Award for Lifetime Contribution to the Arts.

Hans Hollein

To the Austrian Hans Hollein, laureate of the 1985 Pritzker Prize, architecture is always an art. He has described his very personal brand of postmodernism as "pluralistic . . . sometimes lonely and misunderstood, sometimes praised and followed."

Hollein was born in 1934 in Vienna, and studied engineering and fine arts there. He did graduate work at the Illinois Institute of Technology, Chicago, under Ludwig Mies van der Rohe, and at the University of California, Berkeley.

He began his rise to international prominence with his first commission, the twelve-foot-wide Retti Candle Shop in Vienna (1964–65), for which he won the 1966 Reynolds Award. This led to a series of designs for elegant shops, including two exquisitely executed stores for the Viennese jeweler Schullin.

His best-known work, the Municipal Museum in Mönchengladbach, Germany (1972–82), is an elaborate dialogue between landscape and building, a form of industrial modernism erupting from a solid block of stone. In 1990 Hollein completed Haas-Haus, his first large-scale commission in Vienna. The multi-use retail complex faces St. Stephan's Cathedral in the historic heart of the city, and although built of modern materials, the complex echoes the rounded corners of an ancient Roman fort that once stood on the site. Haas-Haus adds yet another layer to the mix of neighboring buildings and styles enriching the city's historic fabric.

Hollein's considerable influence derives as well from his role as lecturer, writer, and designer of exhibitions, furniture, glassware, silverware, and ceramics. Since 1976 he has been head of the School and Institute of Design at the Academy of Applied Arts in Vienna. He has lectured widely and served as visiting professor at Yale University,

Washington University in St. Louis, Missouri, and Ohio State University, Columbus.

Hollein is the recipient of numerous awards, such as the Reynolds Memorial Award in 1966 and 1984, and the Grand Austrian State Award and the German Architecture Award, both in 1983. He is an honorary fellow of the AIA.

Philip Johnson

Born in Cleveland in 1906, Philip Johnson – critic, historian, and architect – received his bachelor's degree in classics from Harvard College in 1927.

Influenced by the European modernist movement, which would also shape his early architectural career, Johnson organized the exhibition *Modern Architecture* at The Museum of Modern Art, New York, in 1932. The show and its catalogue, *The International Style,* written with historian Henry-Russell Hitchcock, introduced the works of Ludwig Mies van der Rohe, Walter Gropius, and Le Corbusier to the American public. Johnson served as director of the Department of Architecture of MoMA from 1930 to 1935. He then returned to Harvard to pursue an architectural degree, and graduated from its School of Design in 1943. Johnson resumed his post at MoMA in 1946 and remained until 1954.

A self-proclaimed "functional eclectic," Johnson has been a dominant force in this century's architectural environment since the completion of his first significant building, the Glass House in New Canaan, Connecticut (1947–49). His collaboration with Mies on the Seagram Building, New York (1954–58), influenced many of his projects in the 1950s and 1960s. The Amon Carter Museum of Modern Art, Fort Worth, Texas (1961), and the East and Garden wings of MoMA (1959–64) exemplify his early dedication to the modernist aesthetic.

The Garden Grove Community Church, California (1977–80, popularly known as the Crystal Cathedral), marked a turning point, one that coincided with the beginning of Johnson's collaboration with

John Burgee, which lasted until 1991. This shift was characterized first by a gradual relaxation of the Miesian vocabulary, as seen in the IDS Center, Minneapolis (1968–73), then an adoption of neoclassicism, as in the Boston Public Library (1966–73), and it culminated in the postmodern design of the AT&T Building, New York (1979–84). In Johnson's recent Gate House at his New Canaan home (1995) he has again proven that he is able to employ yet another architectural vocabulary.

Johnson has been a member of the American Academy of Arts and Letters since 1963. He won the AIA gold medal in 1978 and the Pritzker Prize in 1979. He also holds honorary doctorates from several universities, including Ohio State, the University of Houston, and Yale.

Fumihiko Maki

Within fifty years Fumihiko Maki saw the Tokyo of his childhood transformed from a garden city of low-scale, clay tile structures into an industrial metropolis. He describes the Tokyo of today as "the world's largest assemblage of industrially produced artifacts." The relationship between architecture and the environment is a constant source of inspiration and concern for Maki. "Architecture must be thought of as the link . . . sensitivity to other human beings and human situation – or its lack – will be evident in the resulting architecture."[1]

Maki was born in Tokyo in 1928. He received his undergraduate architectural degree from Tokyo University in 1951. He continued his studies at Cranbrook Academy in Bloomfield Hills, Michigan, and the Graduate School of Design at Harvard University under José Luis Sert. Maki was profoundly influenced by Sert, although traditional Japanese concepts of space and composition would pervade his work as well.

In the Hillside Terrace Apartments, Tokyo, constructed in three stages between 1966 and 1979, Maki faithfully followed the principles of modernism in designing a complex of human scale in unadorned concrete, glass, and metal. In the Central Building at Tsukuba University, completed in 1974, he explored the possibilities of glass block. Used over the entire surface, they manifest a tendency toward what Maki calls "transparent romanticism."

Maki investigated the expressive potential of metal in designs for the Municipal Gymnasium, Fujisawa (1980–84), and the Wocoal Media Center, Tokyo (1982–85). The pleated stainless-steel roof of the gymnasium floats over the arena, linking the earth with the sky. Its form has elicited comparisons to a helmet, a beetle, and a spaceship. The aluminum facade of the Wocoal building is conceived as a collage of a number of elements and represents an attempt to achieve a dynamic equilibrium between "the parts and the whole," which is the basis of Maki's architecture.

Outstanding works of the 1990s include the Center for the Arts in Yerba Buena Gardens Visual Arts Center, San Francisco (1988–93), the Tokyo Church of Christ (completed in 1995), and the Kaze-no-Oka Crematorium in Nakatsu, Oita Prefecture, Japan (1993–97).

Maki was the 1993 winner of the Pritzker Prize. His other awards include the Japan Art Prize (1980), the Reynolds Award (1987), the Wolf Prize for Art (1988), and the Gold Medal of the International Union of Architects (1993). He holds an honorary doctorate from Washington University, St. Louis, Missouri, where he taught for ten years.

1. Fumihiko Maki, "Acceptance Address," *The Pritzker Architecture Prize, 1993: Fumihiko Maki* (Los Angeles: Jensen and Walker, 1993).

Richard Meier

Throughout his career, Richard Meier has maintained a consistency of stylistic choices, which makes his work among the most recognizable in the profession. The recurring use of white cladding and the clarity of composition are unmistakable Meier trademarks.

Meier was born in 1934 in Newark, New Jersey, and received his architectural training at Cornell University, Ithaca, New York. He worked briefly in three New York architectural firms before establishing his own practice in 1963.

Meier was a member of the New York Five, a group of architects who advocated a formalism similar to that of the early modern rationalist architects. He has remained the most constant in his approach throughout his more than thirty-five years of professional practice. Explorations of space, form, and structure, with inspiration traced to the works of Le Corbusier, are evident from his first single-family homes to the recently opened Getty Center in Los Angeles.

One of his first commissions, the Smith House in Darien, Connecticut (1965–67), became the prototype for his many celebrated residences. In them Meier has used contrasts between transparency and solid, curved and rectilinear forms, to delineate public and private spaces. He has developed these concepts further in public buildings, and they echo in houses designed even twenty years later, such as the Ackerberg House, Malibu, California (1984–86).

Museum projects reflect Meier's preoccupation with the use of light to define space. A notable example is the central atrium of the High Museum of Art, Atlanta (1980–83), which Meier described as "a social gathering place." In the Museum für Kunsthandwerk, Frankfurt, Germany (1979–85), he evokes the use of light in the Baroque churches of Germany, where, he says, "light is central to the experiences of the architectural volume."

The centerpiece of a large urban revitalization project, the Hague City Hall and Library, the Netherlands (1986–95), marked Meier's transition to large commissions. Other outstanding European projects include the Exhibition and Assembly Building, Ulm, Germany (1986–93), the Canal + Headquarters in Paris (1988–92), and the Museum of Contemporary Art in Barcelona (1987–95).

The recently completed Getty Center, on a one-hundred-ten-acre site in northern Los Angeles (1984–97), is the largest project Meier has undertaken. Described as architecture of quality and permanence, it appropriately represents the strength and scope of the Getty institution.

In addition to the 1984 Pritzker Prize, Meier has received numerous awards and honors, including the RIBA Gold Medal in 1989, and the AIA Gold Medal and the Praemium Imperiale in 1997.

José Rafael Moneo

José Rafael Moneo was born in 1937 in Tudela, Navarra, Spain. He is the son of an industrial engineer, and his early love of painting and philosophy was diverted to architecture as a result of his father's interest in the subject. As a student at the University of Madrid he worked with architect Francisco Javier de Oiza, and upon completion of his architecture degree in 1961 he assisted Jørn Utzon in Denmark on the design of the Sydney Opera House in Australia (1957–73).

Moneo rose to prominence initially as a teacher and theorist rather than a practitioner. His extensive academic credentials include a two-year fellowship at the Academy of Spain in Rome, which he says was fundamental to his career. He has served on the faculties of the schools of architecture in both Barcelona and Madrid. He was one of the cofounders of the influential magazine *Arquitecturas bis*. During the 1970s and 1980s he became a visiting professor at the schools of architecture of Princeton and Harvard universities, and he was chairman of the Architecture Department of the Harvard Graduate School of Design from 1985 to 1990.

Moneo's architecture is deeply tied to its unique time and place. He speaks with reverence about the significance of the site, "the inevitable first material of any construction," and the necessity for architecture to be relevant to and expressive of its surroundings. Moneo is critical of current theories that encourage a new architecture for a homogeneous world, one that is characterized by the repetition of images regardless of context – an architecture appropriate for the new reality of cyberspace, where "anywhere" exists. In contrast, Moneo's

architecture cannot ignore the concept of place nor the desire to provide the visitor with a wondrous interactive exploration. His knowledge of construction and materials is also great.

Of his numerous critically acclaimed works, the National Museum of Roman Art, Mérida, Spain, completed in 1985, is the most powerful. His contributions to urban transportation in his native country include the Atocha Railway Station in Madrid (1984–92) and the San Pablo Airport in Seville (1987–91). Recent commissions include the Beck Addition to the Museum of Fine Arts, Houston, under construction, and the Museums of Modern Art and Architecture, Stockholm, inaugurated in 1998. He also won the competition to design the new cathedral in Los Angeles.

Moneo was honored in 1992 with the Spanish government's highest award, the Gold Medal for Achievement in the Arts. In 1996 he became the first Spanish architect to win the Pritzker Prize. Also that year he was presented with gold medals by the French Academy of Architecture and the International Union of Architects.

Oscar Niemeyer

In 1988 the tenth Pritzker Prize was awarded to two masters of modernism, Gordon Bunshaft of the United States and Oscar Niemeyer of Brazil. Niemeyer's architecture, conceived as lyrical sculpture, expands on the principles and innovations of Le Corbusier to become a kind of free-form modernism that is uniquely Brazilian.

Niemeyer was born in 1907 in Rio de Janeiro, Brazil, and educated at the Academy of Fine Arts there. In 1938–39 he designed the Brazilian Pavilion for the New York World's Fair; it brought international recognition to Brazilian modernism. His celebrated career began to blossom with his involvement in the project for the Ministry of Education and Health in Rio, completed in 1945. The ministry was the first modernist work of monumental public architecture in Latin America; on it Le Corbusier acted as project consultant to a group of architects headed by Niemeyer's mentor, Lucio Costa. Although the design is essentially Le Corbusier's, Niemeyer emerged from the experience a brilliant designer in his own right.

In 1947 he was invited to participate in the United Nations Headquarters competition. His contribution to the final design and the siting of the building was significant.

In 1956, collaborating once again with Costa, he directed the artistic decision-making in the planning of Brasília, the country's new capital. Brasília's acknowledged aesthetic success resulted largely from the complete accord between Costa's master plan and Niemeyer's architecture.

From 1962 until 1974 Niemeyer worked simultaneously on projects at home and in Europe, Africa, and the Middle East. His most recent accomplishment, an exposition annex for Ibirapuera Park in São Paulo, recalls the ultimate source of his inspiration – the Brazilian landscape.

Niemeyer's awards are many. He has been an honorary member of the American Academy of Arts and Letters since 1964, of the AIA since 1970, and of the RIBA since 1989. He was presented with the gold medals of the French Academy of Architecture and of the RIBA in 1982 and 1998, respectively.

Ieoh Ming Pei

In accepting the 1983 Pritzker Prize, Ieoh Ming Pei described himself as "one of a generation of American architects who built upon the pioneering perceptions of the modern movement with an unwavering conviction in its significant achievements in art, technology, and design." Pei has maintained his faith in modernism and humanized it by bringing to it subtlety, lyricism, and beauty.

I. M. Pei emigrated to the United States from Canton, China, where he was born in 1917. He received his bachelor of architecture degree from the Massachusetts Institute of Technology in 1940 and his master of architecture degree from the Harvard Graduate School of Design, where he studied under Walter Gropius, in 1946. He remained at Harvard for two more years as an assistant professor.

In 1948 Pei joined Webb and Knapp, Inc., in New York, one of the largest developers in the United States. As director of architecture and research, he created architectural opportunities out of commercial situations. Pei established I. M. Pei and Partners in 1955, concentrating primarily on large urban redevelopment projects. That year Pei designed the office tower of the Mile High Center in Denver for Webb and Knapp; it illustrates the extent to which he subscribed to Mies's glass-and-steel formula. Elevated on stilts, as Mies would have advocated, the complex is also the first indication of Pei's career-long penchant for designing handsome open spaces.

In the 1960s Pei shifted away from large-scale redevelopment projects in glass and steel to prestigious commissions for cultural and other institutions in which he could explore the expressive plasticism of sculptural concrete. The breakthrough in this new direction came with his design for the National Center for Atmospheric Research in Boulder, Colorado (1961). Pei was subsequently chosen as the architect for the John F. Kennedy Library (1964) and the East Building of the National Gallery of Art, Washington, D.C. (1968–78).

Pei's remarkable extension of the Louvre in Paris (1983–93) is perhaps his greatest and best known work. In 1989, following the completion of the Louvre pyramid, he renamed his firm Pei Cobb Freed and Partners, an indication of his desire to share responsibility and find the time to pursue projects selected, as he says, for "personal and philosophical reasons." His most recent works include the Morton H. Meyerson Symphony Center in Dallas (1982–89), the Rock and Roll Hall of Fame and Museum in Cleveland (1987–95), and the Miho Museum in Shiga Prefecture, Japan (1991–96).

Pei holds several honorary degrees and is the recipient of numerous awards, including the Brunner Prize in Architecture from the National Institute of Arts and Letters (1961), the gold medals of the AIA (1979) and the French Academy of Architecture (1981), and the Praemium Imperiale (1989).

Renzo Piano

Renzo Piano, the 1998 Pritzker Prize winner, is perhaps best known for his controversial design of the Centre Georges Pompidou, located in the heart of Paris and completed in 1978. Conceived in collaboration with English architect Richard Rogers and described by Piano as "a joyful urban machine . . . a creature that might have come from a Jules Verne book,"[1] Beaubourg, as it is called, has become a cultural icon, expressive of Piano's love of technology.

Born in Genoa in 1937, Piano comes from a family of builders. Following his graduation from Milan Polytechnic Architecture School in 1964, he worked in his father's construction company and later was associated with the offices of Louis Kahn in Philadelphia and Z. S. Mackowsky in London. He formed Renzo Piano Building Workshop in 1980, which now has offices in Paris, Genoa, and Berlin.

Piano is a prolific architect whose wide-ranging repertoire includes a housing complex on the rue de Meaux, Paris (1988–91); the world's largest air terminal, built on a man-made island in Osaka Bay in Japan (1988–94); the conversion of a 1920s Fiat manufacturing plant in Turin into a multi-faceted center for technology and trade fairs (1985–93); and the San Nicola Soccer Stadium in Bari, Italy (1987–90), site of the 1990 World Soccer Championships.

In 1992 he embarked on the $500 million rehabilitation of Genoa's ancient harbor, a gigantic urban reclamation project conceived in celebration of the five hundredth anniversary of the discovery of America. His respect for the character of older cities won him the international competition to develop the master plan for the reconstruction of Potsdamer Platz, which was the center of Berlin's social and cultural life before World War II.

Although best known for vast projects that stretch the limits of technology, Piano is equally recognized for his sensitively designed spaces for art. Two stunning examples are the Menil Collection Museum in Houston (1981–87), a discreet complex of buildings that incorporates an ingenious system of climate and light control, and the exquisitely simple Beyeler Foundation, nestled in the trees near Basel, Switzerland (1993–97). Major works still in progress include the Mercedes Benz Design Center in Stuttgart, a new auditorium for Rome, and the Harvard University Art Museum Master Plan Renovation and Expansion project.

Piano's work has been exhibited internationally. He is the recipient of numerous awards, including the RIBA Gold Medal (1989), the Brunner Prize in Architecture (1994), and the Praemium Imperiale (1995).

1. Renzo Piano, *The Renzo Piano Logbook* (London: Thames and Hudson, 1997), p. 38.

Christian de Portzamparc

The 1994 Pritzker laureate, Christian de Portzamparc, is the youngest architect and the first Frenchman to receive the prize. His architecture has revitalized the urban landscape in France and abroad with an innovative approach to form and space.

The son of a French army officer, Portzamparc was born in Casablanca, Morocco, in 1944 and eventually settled in Marseilles. He graduated from the École Supérieure des Beaux-Arts in 1969 and has achieved recognition as both a painter and an architect. Citing Le Corbusier as the stimulus for his interest in art and subsequent choice of a career in architecture, Portzamparc is a prominent member of a new generation of practitioners who have expanded the tenets of the Beaux-Arts and modernism to create a contemporary aesthetic vocabulary.

Portzamparc's free-form shapes and his colors and textures are a result of his unique approach to the design process. First consideration is given to the functions of the interior space. The exterior enclosure of these relationships can then become a free-style exercise. Through the creation of his "inside and outside places," Portzamparc seeks to alter the way we see and use buildings – to improve our experience of the built world. A sensitive urbanist, Portzamparc envisions the city as a total environment, not the sum of its architectural parts. While acknowledging the architectural heritage of the modern movement, he rejects the wholesale eradication of the history of the urban fabric, which defined the modern theory of city planning.

Portzamparc's first commission was for a water tower in 1969. He based his concept on the idea of the Tower of Babel, and it stands as a monument at a crossroads in the new community of Marne–La Vallée, twenty miles east of Paris. His numerous housing projects have included Les Hautes Formes, Paris (1975–79), and his first international project, in Fukuoka, Japan, completed in 1991.

Portzamparc made a stunning contribution to the worlds of music, dance, and education as part of President François Mitterrand's *Grands Projets* program of new building in Paris. His Cité de la Musique, located in the park of La Villette, on the northern edge of Paris, comprises two structures: the West Building, which houses a concert hall, was finished in 1990, and the East Building, where the conservatory is located, was completed in 1995.

Portzamparc was awarded the Gold Medal of the French Academy of Architecture in 1992 and was made an honorary fellow of the AIA in 1997.

Kevin Roche

"What I have never understood," said Kevin Roche in a 1985 interview, "is architects who write the same poem over and over again, in the same meter and style, even though the subject matter has changed." It is evident from the stark monumentality of his corporate headquarters, including the Ford Foundation Headquarters in New York (1963–68), and the vast neoclassical Bouygues World Headquarters outside Paris (1983–87),

that Roche is the author of some very different poems, indeed.

Born in Dublin, Ireland, in 1922, Roche received his undergraduate degree in architecture from the National University of Dublin in 1945. He continued his studies in 1948 with Ludwig Mies van der Rohe at the Illinois Institute of Technology, Chicago, but left after one semester, disenchanted with the modernist emphasis on architecture's formal vocabulary over its social responsibility. His search for the humanist side of architecture led him to the Bloomfield Hills, Michigan, office of Eliel and Eero Saarinen, where he became right-hand man to Eero in 1950 following Eliel's death.

Roche and John Dinkeloo assumed control of the practice in 1961, when Eero Saarinen died suddenly at the height of his career. After completing some of Saarinen's most famous projects – including the TWA World Flight Center in New York (1956–62), the St. Louis Arch (1959–64), and the headquarters for Deere and Company in Moline, Illinois (1957–63) – they founded, in 1966, Kevin Roche, John Dinkeloo, and Associates. The new firm's first commission was in California, for the Oakland Museum, which they completed in 1968. It is recognized as one of the world's outstanding museum buildings. During the 1970s their many commissions for powerful East Coast corporations included the headquarters for Union Carbide in rural Connecticut (1976–82). Also built during this period was United Nations Plaza One, New York (1969–75), which is considered by some critics as the apotheosis of Roche's skyscraper form; a second tower was built in 1979–83.

Since Dinkeloo's death in 1981 Roche has demonstrated a predilection for an increasingly classical vocabulary, as evidenced in his design for the corporate headquarters for General Foods in Rye, New York (1977–83), and the Leo Burnett Building in Chicago (1985–89). The diversity of his practice and his approach is demonstrated by such projects as the master plan and additions to the Metropolitan Museum of Art, New York (1967–91), including the famous

Egyptian Wing, which was completed in 1982; the towering Northern Telecom Headquarters in Atlanta (1981–86); and the addition to the French Gothic–style building that houses the Jewish Museum in New York (1989–93).

The recipient of the 1982 Pritzker Prize, Roche has been honored by many other architectural and design organizations as well. He won the Brunner Prize in Architecture from the National Institute of Arts and Letters in 1965 and the gold medals of the French Academy of Architecture and the AIA in 1977 and 1983, respectively.

Aldo Rossi

Aldo Rossi was a true Renaissance man, involved in many different aspects of culture: he was an architect, a painter, and a writer. He was born in 1931 in Milan. Rossi served as editor of the architectural magazine *Casabella* from 1955 to 1964 and received his degree in architecture from Milan Polytechnic in 1959. His theoretical writings on what he regarded as the catastrophic state of architecture in the 1960s culminated in the 1966 publication of *The Architecture of the City,* which offered the new generation of architects a unique point of reference for the rediscovery, study, and analysis of the city.

Central to the understanding of Rossi's work is the idea that the tools of the architect consist of learned facts, theories, and systems, combined with all the works of architecture he or she has experienced. While Rossi resolutely believed in the liberation of architecture from the dictates of functionalism, this did not lead to arbitrariness of design; he held that there is always a source in the process of creation. Looking at one of his designs or buildings one is often overcome by a sense of déjà vu, but he could reproduce the essence and character of the past and present without pastiche. His language is direct, his work unmistakable.

The immense reservoir of Rossi's imagination yielded the Teatro del Mondo for the Venice Biennale in 1980. Rossi conceived of a veritable ship, floating on the sea, its tower recalling a lighthouse, a place like a theater where one can be observed as well as observe. Memories of childhood summers by the sea are hinted at in the theater's architecture. In addition to Rossi's many projects in Italy, his major works include the Friedrichstadt Housing Complex, Berlin (1981–88), the Hotel il Palazzo in Fukuoka, Japan (1987–94), and the Bonnefanten Museum in Maastricht, the Netherlands (1990–95). Rossi also became internationally known as a designer of interiors, furniture, and other household objects.

Rossi taught and lectured in the United States and Europe, and had been a professor at the Architecture Institute in Venice since 1976. He was awarded the Pritzker Prize in 1990. Until his untimely death in 1997 at age sixty-six, he continued in his tireless determination toward "a new architecture that supersedes style, a universal architecture."

Alvaro Siza

Deceptively simple in form, the architecture of Alvaro Siza goes beyond its modernist influences to achieve an aesthetic sensitivity unique to the rural or urban context to which it belongs. Siza's reverence for site and respect for context are evident in projects that range from swimming pools to mass-housing developments. He describes his architecture as one of "transformation, not invention."

Siza was born in the small coastal town of Matosinhos, Portugal, in 1933. He completed his studies at the University of Oporto School of Architecture in 1954. During the first three years of private practice he collaborated with Fernando Tavora, and he claims that Alvar Aalto was a strong influence on him at this time. The freedom and freshness of Siza's designs are achieved through the bold use of forms and materials of exquisite simplicity. The connection of the architecture to the landscape, so characteristic of his early projects, is dramatically illustrated in the Swimming Pool Complex in Leça da Palmeira (1961–66), which is nestled into the massive rocks of the Atlantic coast. Later works respond to the surrounding landscape, in some cases creating marked contrasts with it.

As Siza's commissions extended to countries outside Portugal – such as the urban plan and housing development for Schilderswijk, the Hague (1983–88), the Museum of Modern Art in Santiago de Compostela, Spain (1988–93), and the Meteorological Center for the Olympics in Barcelona (1989–92) – he received more international acclaim.

Of the many outstanding low-cost housing units Siza has designed for the government of Portugal, the Malaqueira Quarter project in Evora won him the Prince of Wales Prize in Urban Design from the Harvard University Graduate School of Design in 1988. Siza has been honored by numerous institutions in Europe, including the prestigious Mies van der Rohe Foundation, which recognized him for the Borges and Irmão Bank in Vila do Conde, Portugal (1982–86). He is a member of the faculty of the University of Oporto and has lectured throughout the world.

James Stirling

James Stirling is considered by many as the premier architect of his generation, an unparalleled innovator in postwar international architecture. His untimely death in 1992, at age sixty-six, left an inspired and inspiring body of work that brilliantly underlines the importance of historical continuity and urban context.

Stirling was born in Glasgow in 1926. He was educated at the University of Liverpool School of Architecture and began practice in partnership with James Gowan in London in 1956. Over a seven-year period they designed some of the most significant projects of the time, most notably the garden apartments at Ham Common (1955–58), the seminal Engineering Building at Leicester University (1959–63), and the Cambridge University History Building (1964–67). Stirling's early work pushed

modernity convincingly beyond its accepted boundaries, and from 1970 he moved toward intensified historical imagery and concern with the relationship of the building to the urban fabric.

In 1971 Stirling began to work in association with Michael Wilford. From this point on, the scale and number of his projects broadened to include museums, galleries, libraries, and theaters, perhaps the most significant being his competition-winning design for the Neue Staatsgalerie in Stuttgart (1977–84). This provocative building incorporates many references assembled in an unconventional way and thus encourages the visitor to constantly reevaluate it.

Among his late complete works are the Braun Research and Production Headquarters in Melsungen, Germany (1986–92), and a bookshop in the Biennale Gardens, Venice (1989–91).

Stirling was knighted just twelve days before his death. He had been awarded the world's major architectural prizes – the Alvar Aalto Medal in 1977, the RIBA Gold Medal in 1980, the Pritzker Prize in 1981, and the Praemium Imperiale in 1990. He taught in Europe and served as Charles Davenport Professor at Yale University from 1967 until his death.

Kenzo Tange

Kenzo Tange, winner of the 1987 Pritzker Prize, is one of Japan's most highly honored architects. Teacher, writer, architect, and urban planner, he is revered not only for his own work but also for his influence on younger architects, namely Arata Isozaki, Kisho Kurokawa, and Fumihiko Maki.

Tange was born in Shikoku Island, in the south of Japan, in 1913 and educated at the University of Tokyo in the 1930s and 1940s. His work of the postwar years, epitomized in the Hiroshima Peace Center (1946–94), communicates a deep understanding of traditional culture while "assuming the importance of a signpost at the moment when a modern style was being sought in the architecture of Japan." Tange is perhaps best known for his 1964 National Gymnasiums and his 1960 plan for Tokyo, which proposed an urban design solution to the pressures of growth by creating man-made islands in Tokyo Bay that would carry megastructures and a complex communication system. In 1966 he completed the Yamanashi Press and Broadcasting Center in Kofu, a complex that houses three firms in different but related fields. As in the Tokyo Plan, with this project Tange once again succeeded in realizing a new concept of urban architecture in a building conceived not as a fixed, unalterable form but one that could be modified as the need arose.

Tange has designed works in more than twenty countries, including two notable contributions in the United States: the Arts Complex for the Minneapolis Society of Fine Arts (1970–74) and the American Medical Association Headquarters in Chicago (1983–90).

He holds three architectural gold medals – those of the RIBA (1965), the AIA (1966), and the French Academy of Architecture (1973). In 1993 he won the Praemium Imperiale and in 1996 was made a member of the Order of the Legion of Honor of France.

Robert Venturi

In 1991 Robert Venturi was awarded the Pritzker Prize for his theoretical writing as well as his architecture. His pivotal book, *Complexity and Contradiction in Architecture* (1966), was cited by the jury for directing the mainstream of architecture away from modernism and was praised by Vincent Scully as "probably the most important writing on the making of architecture since Le Corbusier's *Vers une Architecture* of 1923."

Venturi was born in Philadelphia in 1925 and received bachelor's and master's degrees in architecture from Princeton University. His education, with its emphasis on architectural history, was reinforced by a Rome Prize fellowship at the American Academy in the mid-1950s. In Italy, Venturi became fascinated by mannerist architec-

ture – its contrasts in scale, its surprises, its deviations from classical norms – and he would dwell on these tendencies in an early project for which he first achieved public acclaim, a house for his mother, completed in 1964. It received the AIA Twenty-five Year Award and is acknowledged by Venturi as a testing ground for ideas that he would refine in later work. Although a generation of architects borrowed freely from its design, that same generation was at a loss to reproduce the house's carefully modified scale, intricate layering of space and materials, and contradictory quirkiness. While Venturi concedes that much of postmodernism's basis corresponds to his thinking, his work goes beyond its surface effects. Each of his buildings adapts to and interprets its surroundings, accepting the validity and relevance of mass culture to architecture through symbolic references. The publication of Venturi's controversial book *Learning from Las Vegas* in 1972, written with Denise Scott Brown and Steven Izenour, placed him outside the traditional categories for labeling architectural styles and movements.

From the little house that became an icon to such notable works as the Allen Memorial Art Museum in Oberlin, Ohio (1973–76), Gordon Wu Hall at Princeton University (1980–83), and the Sainsbury Wing addition to Britain's National Gallery of Art (1986–91), this architecture surprises, provokes, and above all teaches us to look at the built environment with new eyes.

Venturi is the recipient of honorary doctorates from Yale University, Princeton, Oberlin College, the University of Pennsylvania, Bard College, and New Jersey Institute of Technology, and he has been honored with numerous architecture and design awards.

Bibliography

Tadao Ando

Ando, Tadao. *Tadao Ando,* exh. cat. Paris: Centre de Création Industrielle, Centre Georges Pompidou, 1993.

Dal Co, Francesco. *Tadao Ando: Complete Works.* London: Phaidon, 1995.

Fields, Darell Wayne. *Tadao Ando: Dormant Lines.* New York: Rizzoli, 1991.

Frampton, Kenneth. *Tadao Ando: The Yale Studio and Current Works.* New York: Rizzoli, 1989.

————. *Tadao Ando,* exh. cat. New York: The Museum of Modern Art, 1991.

Frampton, Kenneth, ed. *Tadao Ando: Buildings, Projects, Writings.* New York: Rizzoli, 1984.

Furuyama, Masao. *Tadao Ando.* Zürich: Artemis, 1993.

Futagawa, Yukio, ed. *Tadao Ando.* GA Architect series, vol. 8. Tokyo: A.D.A. Edita, 1987.

————. *Tadao Ando.* GA Document Extra series, vol. 1. Tokyo: A.D.A. Edita, 1995.

Tadao Ando. Architectural Monograph series, vol. 14. London: Academy, 1990.

Zardini, Mirko, ed. *Rokko Housing.* Quaderni di Casabella series. Milan: Electa, Nov. 1986.

Luis Barragán

Ambasz, Emilio. *The Architecture of Luis Barragán.* New York: The Museum of Modern Art, 1976.

Anda Alanis, Enrique de. *Luis Barragán: Clásico del silencio.* Bogotá: Escala, 1989.

Barragán, Luis. *Capilla en Tlalpan, Ciudad de México, 1952.* Mexico City: Sirio, 1980.

Buendia Julbez, José María, et al. *The Life and Work of Luis Barragán.* New York: Rizzoli, 1997.

Riggen Martínez, Antonio. *Luis Barragán: Mexico's Modern Master, 1902–1988.* New York: Monacelli, 1996.

Rispa, Raul, ed. *Barragán: The Complete Works.* New York: Princeton Architectural Press, 1996.

Saito, Yutaka. *Luis Barragán.* Mexico City: Noriega, 1994.

Salas Portugal, Armando. *Photographs of the Architecture of Luis Barragán.* New York: Rizzoli, 1992.

San Martin, Ignacio, ed. *Luis Barragán: The Phoenix Papers.* Tempe, Ariz.: Center for Latin American Studies Press, 1997.

Gottfried Böhm

Böhm, Gottfried. *WDR Arkaden.* Cologne: Oktagon, 1997.

Darius, Veronika. *Der Architekt Gottfried Böhm: Bauten der Sechziger Jahre.* Düsseldorf: Beton, 1988.

Feldmeyer, Gerhard. *The New German Architecture.* New York: Rizzoli, 1993.

Pehnt, Wolfgang. *Expressionist Architecture.* New York: Praeger, 1973.

Raev, Svetlozar, ed. *Gottfried Böhm: Bauten und Projekte, 1950–1980.* Cologne: Krämer, 1982.

Gordon Bunshaft

Danz, Ernst. *Architecture of Skidmore, Owings, and Merrill, 1950–1962.* New York: Praeger, 1963.

Drexler, Arthur. *Architecture of Skidmore, Owings, and Merrill, 1963–1973.* London: Architectural Press, 1974.

————. *Three New Skyscrapers.* New York: The Museum of Modern Art, 1983.

Heyer, Paul. *Architects on Architecture: New Directions in America.* New York: Walker, 1978.

Krinsky, Carol Herselle. *Gordon Bunshaft of Skidmore, Owings, and Merrill.* New York and Cambridge, Mass.: Architectural History Foundation and M.I.T. Press, 1988.

Peter, John. *Masters of Modern Architecture.* New York: Braziller, 1958.

Sverre Fehn

Fjeld, Per Olaf. *Sverre Fehn: The Thought of Construction.* New York: Rizzoli, 1983.

Gronvold, Ulf, and Sverre Fehn. "Sverre Fehn." *Byggekunst: The Norwegian Reveiw of Architecture,* vol. 74, no. 2 (1992): 76–127.

Norbert-Schulz, Christian. *Sverre Fehn: Opera completa.* Milan: Electa, 1997.

Norri, Marja-Riitta, and Maija Kärkkäinen, eds. *Sverre Fehn: The Poetry of the Straight Line.* Helsinki: Suomen Rakennustaiteen Museo, 1992.

Postiglione, Gennaro. *I Musei di Sverre Fehn.* Naples: University of Naples, 1996.

Frank O. Gehry

Arnell, Peter, and Ted Bickford, eds. *Frank Gehry, Buildings and Projects.* New York: Rizzoli, 1985.

Bletter, Rosemarie Haag, et al. *The Architecture of Frank Gehry.* Minneapolis and New York: Walker Art Center and Rizzoli, 1986.

Bossiere, Oliver, and Martin Filler. *The Vitra Design Museum: Frank Gehry, Architect.* New York: Rizzoli, 1990.

Celant, Germano. *Il Corso del Coltello/The Course of the Knife: Claes Oldenburg, Coosje van Bruggen, Frank O. Gehry.* New York: Rizzoli, 1987.

Forster, Kurt W., et al. *Frank O. Gehry: The Complete Works.* New York: Monacelli, 1998.

Frank O. Gehry: European Projects. Berlin: Aedes, 1994.

Futagawa, Yukio, ed. *Frank O. Gehry.* GA Architect series, vol. 10. Tokyo: A.D.A. Edita, 1993.

Gehry, Frank, et al. *California Aerospace Museum.* London: Phaidon, 1994.

Jencks, Charles, ed. *Frank O. Gehry: Individual Imagination and Cultural Conservatism.* London: Academy, 1995.

Steele, James. *Schnabel House: Frank Gehry.* Architecture in Detail series. London: Phaidon, 1993.

van Bruggen, Coosje. *Frank O. Gehry, Guggenheim Museum Bilbao.* New York: Guggenheim Museum, 1998.

Hans Hollein

Hans Hollein. A + U Extra Edition. Tokyo: A + U, Feb. 1985.

Hollein, Hans. *Hans Hollein: Métaphores et métamorphoses,* exh. cat. Paris: Centre de Création Industrielle, Centre Georges Pompidou, 1987.

Hollein, Hans, and Catherine Cooke, eds. *Vienna Dream and Reality: A Celebration of the Hollein Installations for the Exhibition "Traum und Wirklichkeit, Wien 1870–1930" in the Künstlerhaus Vienna.* London: Architectural Design, 1986.

Pettena, Gianni. *Hans Hollein: Opere 1960–1988.* Milan: Idea Books, 1988.

Sechs Architekten vom Schillerplatz. Vienna: Akademie der Bildenden Künste and Tusch, 1977.

von Scholer, Andreas, et al. *Hans Hollein: Museum für Moderne Kunst, Frankfurt-am-Main.* Berlin: Ernst und Son, 1991.

Philip Johnson

Blake, Peter. *Philip Johnson.* Basel and Boston: Birkhäuser, 1996.

Cappellieri, Alba. *Philip Johnson dall' International Style al Decostruttivismo.* Naples: CLEAN, 1996.

Hitchcock, Henry Russell, and Philip Johnson. *The New International Style.* New York: Norton, 1966. Reprint of *The International Style: Architecture since 1922.* New York: Norton, 1932.

Jacobus, John M. *Philip Johnson.* New York: Braziller, 1962.

Johnson, Philip. *Philip Johnson: Architecture 1949–1965.* New York: Holt, Rinehart, and Winston, 1966.

Kipnis, Jeffrey. *Philip Johnson: Recent Work.* London: Academy, 1996.

Knight, Carleton. *Philip Johnson/John Burgee: Architecture 1979–1985.* New York: Rizzoli, 1985.

Schulze, Franz. *Philip Johnson: Life and Work.* Chicago: University of Chicago Press, 1996.

Whitney, David, and Jeffrey Kipnis, eds. *Philip Johnson: The Glass House.* New York: Pantheon, 1993.

Fumihiko Maki

Banham, Reyner. *Megastructures: Urban Futures of the Recent Past.* New York: Harper and Row, 1976.

Frampton, Kenneth. *A New Wave of Japanese Architecture.* New York: Institute for Architecture and Urban Studies, 1978.

"Fumihiko Maki," special issue of *The Japan Architect,* Mar. 1983.

Fumihiko Maki: A Presence Called Architecture – Report from the Site. Tokyo: TOTO Shuppan, 1996.

"Fumihiko Maki: Maki and Associates," special issue of *The Japan Architect,* Aug./Sept. 1990.

"Fumihiko Maki, 1979–1986," special issue of *Space Design,* Jan. 1986.

Maki, Fumihiko. *Investigations in Collective Form.* St. Louis: School of Architecture, Washington University, 1964.

Maki, Fumihiko, and Associates. *Fumihiko Maki: Buildings and Projects.* New York: Princeton Architectural Press, 1997.

Ross, Michael Franklin. *Beyond Metabolism: The New Japanese Architecture.* New York: Architectural Record Books, 1978.

Salat, Serge. *Fumihiko Maki: An Aesthetic of Fragmentation.* New York: Rizzoli, 1988.

Richard Meier

Ames, Anthony. *Five Houses, 1976–1986.* New York: Princeton Architectural Press, 1988.

Blaser, Werner. *Buildings for Art.* Basel and Boston: Birkhäuser, 1990.

Brawne, Michael. *Museum für Kunsthandwerk: Richard Meier.* Architecture in Detail series. London: Phaidon, 1993.

Flagge, Ingeborg, and Oliver Hamm, eds. *Richard Meier in Europe.* Berlin: Ernst und Sohn, 1997.

Frampton, Kenneth, and Joseph Rykwert. *Richard Meier, Architect: 1985–1991.* New York: Rizzoli, 1991.

Goldberger, Paul. *Richard Meier Houses, 1962–1997.* New York: Rizzoli, 1996.

Jodidio, Philip. *Richard Meier.* Cologne: Taschen, 1995.

Meier, Richard. *Building the Getty.* New York: Knopf, 1997.

Rykwert, Joseph. *Richard Meier, Architect: 1964–1984.* New York: Rizzoli, 1984.

Sack, Manfred. *Richard Meier: Stadthaus Ulm.* Opus series, vol. 9. Berlin: Menges, 1995.

José Rafael Moneo

Colquhoun, Alan, et al. "Rafael Moneo 1986–1992," special issue of *Arquitectura y vivienda* (Madrid), vol. 36, 1992.

Dal Co, Francesco, et al. "Special Feature: Rafael Moneo." *A+U* (Tokyo), no. 227, Aug. 1989.

Levene, Richard C., and Fernando Márquez Cecilia, eds. "Rafael Moneo, 1990–1994," special issue of *El Croquis* (Madrid), vol. 64, 1994.

Moneo, José Rafael. *Fundación Pilar y Joan Miró.* Almeria: Colegio de Arquitectos en Almeria, 1996.

Moneo, José Rafael, and Johan Mårtelius. *Modern Museum and Swedish Museum of Architecture in Stockholm.* Stockholm: Arkitektur Förlag and Raster Förlag, 1998.

Nigst, Peter. *Rafael Moneo: Bauen für die Stadt.* Stuttgart: Hatje, 1993.

Saliga, Pauline, and Martha Thorne, eds. *Building in a New Spain.* Madrid: Ministry of Public Works and Transports, 1992.

Oscar Niemeyer

Botey, Josep M. *Oscar Niemeyer.* Barcelona: Gustavo Gili, 1996.

Fundacio Caixa Barcelona. *Oscar Niemeyer.* Barcelona: Collegi d'Arquitectes de Catalunya, 1990.

"Oscar Niemeyer, 50 años de arquitectura," special issue of *Modulo* (Rio de Janeiro), vol. 97, 1988.

Oscar Niemeyer, 1937–1997. Tokyo: TOTO Shuppan, 1997.

Papadaki, Stamo. *Oscar Niemeyer.* New York: Braziller, 1960.

Petit, Jean. *Niemeyer: Poète d'architecture.* Paris: Bibliothèque des Arts, 1994.

Puppi, Lionello. *Guida a Niemeyer.* Milan: Mondadori, 1987.

———. *Oscar Niemeyer: 1907.* Rome: Officina Edizioni, 1996.

Spade, Rupert. *Oscar Niemeyer.* London: Thames and Hudson, 1971.

Underwood, David Kendrick. *Oscar Niemeyer and Brazilian Free-form Modernism.* New York: Braziller, 1994.

———. *Oscar Niemeyer and the Architecture of Brazil.* New York: Rizzoli, 1994.

Yamaki, Humberto, ed. *Modern Brazilian Architecture.* Tokyo: Process Architecture, 1980.

I. M. Pei

Betsky, Aaron, and Tom Bonner. *Architecture and Medicine: I. M. Pei Designs the Kirkin Clinic.* Birmingham, Ala.: University Press of America, 1993.

Cannell, Michael T. *I. M. Pei: Mandarin of*

Modernism. New York: Carol Southern, 1995.

Chaine, Catherine. *Le Grand Louvre du Donjuan à la pyramide.* Paris: Hatier, 1989.

Diamonstein, Barbaralee. *American Architecture Now.* New York: Rizzoli, 1980.

Reed, Aileen. *I. M. Pei.* Edison, N.Y.: Knickerbocker, 1998.

Suner, Bruno. *Pei.* Paris: Hazan, 1988.

Wiseman, Carter. *I. M. Pei: A Profile in American Architecture.* New York: Abrams, 1990.

Renzo Piano

Bordaz, Robert. *Entretiens.* Paris: Cercle d'Art, 1997.

Buchanan, Peter. *Renzo Piano Building Workshop: Complete Works.* London: Phaidon, 1997.

Lampugnani, Vittorio Magnago, and Renzo Piano. *Renzo Piano, Progetti e architetture, 1987–1994.* Milan: Electa, 1994.

Miotto, Luciana. *Renzo Piano.* Paris: Centre Georges Pompidou, 1987.

Piano, Renzo. *Antico e bello: Il Recupero della città.* Rome and Bari: Laterza, 1980.

Renzo Piano: Progetti e architetture, 1984–1986. Milan: Electa, 1986.

Renzo Piano Building Workshop, 1964–1988. A + U Extra Edition. Tokyo: A + U, Mar. 1989.

Christian de Portzamparc

Euralille – The Making of a New City: Koolhaas, Nouvel, Portzamparc, Viasconti, Duthilleul, Architects. Basel and Boston: Birkhäuser, 1996.

Futagawa, Yukio, ed. *Christian de Portzamparc.* GA Document Extra Series, vol. 4. Tokyo: A.D.A. Edita, 1995.

Jacques, Michel. *Christian de Portzamparc.* Bordeaux, Basel, and Boston: Arc en Rêve Centre d'Architecture and Birkhäuser, 1996.

Le Dantec, Jean-Pierre. *Christian de Portzamparc.* Paris: Editions du Regard, 1995.

Portzamparc, Christian de. *Trois Architectes français: Henri Ciriani, Henri Gaudin, et Christian de Portzamparc,* exh. cat. Paris:

Electa Moniteur, 1984.

———. *Christian de Portzamparc: Scènes d'atelier,* exh. cat. Paris: Centre Georges Pompidou, 1996.

———. *Genealogy des Formes = Genealogy of Forms.* Paris: Dis Voir, 1996.

Portzamparc, Christian de, Maarten Kloos, and Francis Rambert. *Christian de Portzamparc.* Basel and Boston: Birkhäuser, 1996.

Kevin Roche

Dal Co, Francesco, ed. *Kevin Roche.* New York: Rizzoli, 1985.

Johnson, Philip, and John Cook. *Conversations with Architects: Philip Johnson, Kevin Roche, Paul Rudolph, Bertrand Goldberg, Morris Lapidus, Louis Kahn, Charles Moore, Robert Venturi.* New York: Holt, Reinhart, and Winston, 1975.

Kevin Roche. A + U Extra Edition. Tokyo: A + U, Aug. 1987.

Kevin Roche, John Dinkeloo, and Associates, 1962–1975. New York: Hasting House, 1977.

Aldo Rossi

Adjmi, Morris, ed. *Aldo Rossi: Architecture, 1981–1991.* New York: Princeton Architectural Press, 1991.

Adjmi, Morris, and Giovanni Bertolotto, eds. *Aldo Rossi: Drawings and Paintings.* New York: Princeton Architectural Press, 1993.

Arnell, Peter, and Ted Bickford, eds. *Aldo Rossi: Buildings and Projects.* New York: Rizzoli, 1985.

Braghieri, Gianni. *Aldo Rossi.* Barcelona: Gustavo Gili, 1991.

Brusatin, Manlio, and Alberto Prandi, eds. *Aldo Rossi, Teatro del Mondo.* Venice: CLUVA, 1982.

Ferlenga, Alberto. *Aldo Rossi: Architetture, 1988–1992.* Milan: Electa, 1992.

Frampton, Kenneth, ed. *Aldo Rossi in America, 1976 to 1979.* New York: Institute for Architecture and Urban Studies, 1979.

Geisert, Helmut, ed. *Aldo Rossi, Architect.* London: Academy, 1994.

Moschini, Francesco, ed. *Aldo Rossi, progetti*

e disegni, 1962–1979. New York: Rizzoli, 1979.

O'Regan, John, ed. *Aldo Rossi, Selected Writings and Projects.* London: Architectural Design, 1983.

Rossi, Aldo. *The Architecture of the City.* Cambridge, Mass.: M.I.T. Press, 1982.

———. *Il Libro azzurro: I miei progetti, 1981.* Zürich: Jamileh Weber Galerie, 1983.

Savi, Vittorio. *L'Architettura di Aldo Rossi.* Milan: Angeli, 1976.

Alvaro Siza

Alvaro Siza 1954–1988. A + U Extra Edition. Tokyo: A + U, June 1989.

Alvaro Siza professione poetica. Quaderni di Lotus, vol. 6. Milan: Electa, 1986.

Alvaro Siza: Architectures, 1980–1990, exh. cat. Paris: Centre de Création Industrielle, Centre Georges Pompidou, 1990.

Dos Santos, José Paolo, ed. *Alvaro Siza: Works and Projects, 1954–1992.* Barcelona: Gustavo Gili, 1994.

Fleck, Brigitte. *Alvaro Siza.* Basel and Boston: Birkhäuser, 1992.

Rodrigues, Jacinto. *Alvaro Siza: Obra e metodo.* Oporto: Civilizaçao, 1992.

Siza, Alvaro. *El Chiado Lisboa: La Estrategia de la memoria.* Granada, Spain: Delegación en Granada del Colegio de Arquitectos, Sociedad de Lisboa 94, Junta de Andalucia, Consejeria de Obras Públicas y Transportes, 1994.

Testa, Peter. *The Architecture of Alvaro Siza.* Cambridge, Mass.: M.I.T. Dept. of Architecture, 1984.

Trigueiros, Luiz, ed. *Alvaro Siza, 1986–1995.* Lisbon: Blau, 1995.

Wang, Wilfried, ed. *Alvaro Siza, Figures and Configurations: Buildings and Projects, 1986–1988.* Cambridge, Mass., and New York: Harvard University Graduate School of Design and Rizzoli, 1988.

Wang, Wilfried, et al. *Alvaro Siza, City Sketches.* Basel and Boston: Birkhäuser, 1994.

James Stirling

Arnell, Peter, and Ted Bickford, eds. *James Stirling, Buildings and Projects: James Stirling, Michael Wilford, and Associates.* New York: Rizzoli, 1984.

Jacobus, James. *James Stirling: Buildings and Projects, 1950–1974.* New York: Oxford University Press, 1975.

James Stirling and Michael Wilford. Architectural Monographs series, vol. 32. London: Academy, 1993.

Jenkins, David. *Clore Gallery and Tate Gallery, Liverpool: James Stirling, Michael Wilford, and Associates.* Architecture in Detail series. London: Phaidon, 1992.

McKean, John. *Leicester University Engineering Building: James Stirling and James Gowan.* Architecture in Detail series. London: Phaidon, 1994.

Papadakis, Andreas, ed. *James Stirling, Michael Wilford, and Associates.* Architectural Design Profile. London: St. Martins, 1991.

Recent Works of James Stirling, Michael Wilford and Associates, A + U Extra Edition. Tokyo: A + U, May 1990.

Sudjic, Deyan. *Norman Foster, Richard Rogers, James Stirling: New Directions in British Architecture.* London: Thames and Hudson, 1987.

Wilford, Michael, et al. *James Stirling, Michael Wilford, and Associates: Buildings and Projects, 1975–1992.* London: Thames and Hudson, 1994.

Kenzo Tange

Altherr, Alfred. *Three Japanese Architects: Mayekawa, Tange, Sakakura.* New York: Architectural Book Publishing, 1968.

Bettinotti, Massimo, ed. *Kenzo Tange, 1946–1996: Architecture and Urban Design.* Milan: Electa, 1997.

Boyd, Robin. *Kenzo Tange.* New York: Braziller, 1962.

Kultermann, Udo, ed. *Kenzo Tange, 1946–1969: Architecture and Urban Design.* New York: Praeger, 1970.

Moneo, José Rafael. *The Solitude of Buildings: Kenzo Tange Lecture, March 9, 1985.* Cambridge, Mass.: Harvard Graduate School of Design, 1985.

Riani, Paolo. *Kenzo Tange.* New York: Crown, 1969.

Tange, Kenzo. *Genitsu to Sozo: Kenzo Tange, 1946–1958*. Tokyo: Bijutsu Shuppansha, 1966.

Tange, Kenzo, and Noboru Kawazoe. *Ise, Prototype of Japanese Architecture.* Cambridge, Mass.: M.I.T. Press, 1965.

von der Muhll, H. R., ed. *Kenzo Tange.* Bologna: Zanichelli, 1979.

Robert Venturi

Davies, Hugh Marlais, and Anne Farrell. *Learning from La Jolla: Robert Venturi Remakes a Museum in the Precinct of Irving Gill.* La Jolla, Calif.: Museum of Contemporary Art, San Diego, 1998.

Mead, Christopher, ed. *The Architecture of Robert Venturi.* Albuquerque: University of New Mexico Press, 1989.

Schwartz, Frederic, ed. *Mother's House: The Evolution of Vanna Venturi's House in Chestnut Hill.* New York: Rizzoli, 1992.

Venturi, Robert. *Complexity and Contradiction in Architecture.* New York: The Museum of Modern Art, 1966.

——. *Iconography and Electronics upon a Generic Architecture: A View from the Drafting Room.* Cambridge, Mass.: M.I.T. Press, 1996.

Venturi, Robert, and Denise Scott Brown. *View from the Campidoglio: Selected Essays 1953–1984.* New York: Icon, 1985.

Venturi, Robert, Denise Scott Brown, and Steven Izenour. *Learning from Las Vegas.* Cambridge, Mass.: M.I.T. Press, 1972.

Venturi, Scott Brown, and Associates on Houses and Housing. Architectural Monographs series, vol. 21. London: Academy, 1992.

von Moos, Stanislaus. *Venturi, Rauch, and Scott Brown, Buildings and Projects.* New York: Rizzoli, 1987.

Acknowledgments

The efforts required to bring to fruition this major publication and exhibition have been substantial and reflect the contributions of many individuals to whom I am indeed grateful. Those who gave their advice, energy, ideas, and time to this project deserve more thanks than can be conveyed in these brief words. Nonetheless, I wish to express my gratitude and appreciation first of all to Bill Lacy, whose thoughtful counsel, along with that of J. Carter Brown and Ada Louise Huxtable, proved most helpful in defining the project and keeping it on track.

Sincere thanks are in order for the architects who have won the Pritzker Architecture Prize and for the many people in their offices who contributed to this book and exhibition with their time and ideas and provided necessary documents from their archives. In addition, the Barragán Foundation of Birsfelden, Switzerland; the Staatsgalerie Stuttgart; the office of Michael Wilford and Associates, London; the offices of SOM in Chicago and New York; and Morris Adjmi's Studio di Architettura, New York, generously participated in this project in the regrettable absence of Luis Barragán, James Stirling, Gordon Bunshaft, and Aldo Rossi.

The authors, who have so carefully undertaken their texts, deserve particular recognition for analyzing the state of the art of late-twentieth-century architecture. Thanks also go to the photographers who have conscientiously documented the important works included here. A special word of appreciation is due Diana Murphy and Judy Hudson of Abrams for their creativity and constant care in editing, designing, and producing this volume.

For the exhibition of the works of the laureates at the Art Institute of Chicago, Carlos Jiménez has created an inspiring installation. Many departments from the museum – Art Installation, Museum Registration, Physical Plant, Public Affairs, and Publications – have also contributed their services in a most professional way.

Within the Department of Architecture, Carole Merrill diligently prepared the architects' biographies and Lawrence Ebelle-Ebanda assembled the bibliography. All my departmental colleagues provided enthusiasm and assistance every step of the way.

Finally, Jay and Cindy Pritzker must be cited not only for their support of this publication and exhibition but also for their generosity in establishing the Pritzker Architecture Prize. Their vision and concern for the built environment, as reflected through the prize, are unique and unparalleled.

Martha Thorne
Associate Curator of Architecture
The Art Institute of Chicago

Index

Photograph Credits

Courtesy the office of Tadao Ando, 157 top; Sina Baniahmad, courtesy Studio Hollein, 89, 90 top, 91 bottom, 93 top; Barragán Foundation, Switzerland, 61 top; Luc Bernard, courtesy Studio Hollein, 92 bottom right; Tom Bernard, courtesy Venturi, Scott Brown, and Associates, Ltd., Architects, 135 top and right; Dida Biggi, 161, 162 bottom, 163 top right and bottom right; courtesy the office of Gottfried Böhm, 43 top, 94–99; Brecht-Einzig, Ltd., courtesy Michael Wilford and Partners, Ltd., 40, 68 bottom; Richard Bryant/ARCAID, courtesy Michael Wilford and Partners, Ltd., 68 top, 69; Barbara Burg/ Oliver Schuh, courtesy Aldo Rossi Studio di Architettura, 125, 127 top left and bottom; © Roberto Collovà, 34; Jerry Cooke, courtesy Skidmore, Owings, and Merrill, 108 left; Stephanie Courturier/Archipress, 79 top right; Marlies Darsow, courtesy Studio Hollein, 92 top; M. Denance, courtesy Renzo Piano Building Workshop, 176 top and right, 177 top left; ESTO, courtesy Skidmore, Owings, and Merrill, 108 top; courtesy Guy Fehn, 48; © Scott Frances/ ESTO, courtesy Richard Meier and Partners, 31, 82, 83, 84 right, 85, 86 top and bottom; courtesy Frank O. Gehry Associates, 122 top and right, 123 top right and left; Alexandre Georges, courtesy Skidmore, Owings, and Merrill, 110 bottom; Tim Griffith/ESTO, 172, 173; David Heald, © The Solomon R. Guggenheim Foundation, New York, 119, 120 top and left, 121 top and right; David Hirsch, courtesy Venturi, Scott Brown, and Associates, Ltd., Architects, 30 top; © Wolfgang Hoyt, 27 top; Franz Hubman, courtesy Studio Hollein, 42; © Timothy Hursley, 81 top and right; *The Japan Architect*, courtesy Venturi, Scott Brown, and Associates, Ltd., Architects, 133 bottom right; Kawasumi Architectural Photography, courtesy Venturi, Scott Brown, and Associates, Ltd., Architects, 130, 131, 132 top, 133 top; Toshiharu Kitajima, courtesy the office of Fumihiko Maki, 143, 144 left and bottom, 145, 147 left and bottom; Hiroshi Kobayashi, courtesy the office of Tadao Ando, 158 left and bottom; Rollin R. LaFrance, courtesy Venturi, Scott Brown, and Associates, Ltd., Architects, 134 top and left; Arthur Lavine, courtesy Skidmore, Owings, and Merrill, 110 left; Nathaniel Lieberman, courtesy Pei Cobb Freed and Partners, 78 top, 80 top; Duccio Malagamba, 47, 164 center and bottom, 165 top and bottom; Mitsuo Matsuoka, courtesy the office of Tadao Ando, 33 bottom, 155, 156 bottom, 157 right, 159 top; © Peter Mauss/ ESTO, 44 left; Michael Moran Photography, courtesy Philip Johnson, 52–55; Shigeyuri Morishita, courtesy Renzo Piano Building Workshop, 175 right; Osamu Murai, courtesy Kenzo Tange Associates, 33 top, 46 left, 100, 101, 102 top, 103, 104 top and right, 105 top; Thomas H. Murtaugh, courtesy Skidmore, Owings, and Merrill, 109 top; courtesy Neue Staatsgalerie, 67 top; courtesy the office of Oscar Niemeyer, 43 bottom, 112–17; Shigeo Ogawa, courtesy the office of Tadao Ando, 159 right; Tomio Ohashi, courtesy the office of Tadao Ando, 158 right; © Richard Payne, 28, 56, 57; Benoit Perrin, courtesy Pei Cobb Freed and Partners, 76; courtesy Renzo Piano Building Workshop, 35; courtesy the office of Christian de Portzamparc, 46 right, 148–52; C. Richters, courtesy Renzo Piano Building Workshop, 177 top; courtesy Kevin Roche, John Dinkeloo, and Associates, 41, 70–75; Juan Rodríguez, courtesy the office of Alvaro Siza, 138 top and right; Ruiz de Azua, 25; Armando Salas Portugal, courtesy Barragán Foundation, Switzerland, 27 left, 58–63; Diede von Schawen, courtesy Pei Cobb Freed and Partners, 79 left; Shinkenchiku-sha, courtesy the office of Fumihiko Maki, 146 top and center left; courtesy the office of Alvaro Siza, 136, 137, 140, 141; © Terje Solvang, 169 top, 170 top; James L. Stanfield/ National Geographic Image Collection, 77; © Ezra Stoller/ESTO, 106, 107, 111; © Ezra Stoller/ ESTO, courtesy Richard Meier and Partners, 86 left, 87 top and bottom; © Ezra Stoller/ESTO, courtesy Pei Cobb Freed and Partners, 30 bottom; © Ezra Stoller/ESTO, courtesy Skidmore, Owings, and Merrill, 109 bottom, 110 top; Rex Stucky, 21 bottom; courtesy Studio di Architettura, 124, 126, 128, 129; courtesy Kenzo Tange Associates, 105 bottom; Teigens Fotoatelier A.S., 167, 168 left and bottom, 169 bottom right, 171 bottom right; W. Vassal, courtesy Renzo Piano Building Workshop, 175 bottom; Peter Walser, 65, 66 top and center; © 1990 Paul Warchol, 80 left and bottom; courtesy Michael Wilford and Partners, Ltd., 66 bottom; Alfred Wolf, courtesy Pei Cobb Freed and Partners, 79 bottom; John Zukowsky, 139 top.